BLOOMER'S

Developmental
Neuropsychological
Assessments (DNA)

Assessing Basic Executive Learning Processes

Volume I

Individual Response Speed

Richard H. Bloomer Ed. D. M.S. ABPS, FACAPP, FACFEI
Certified Neuro-psychologist
Emeritus Professor
The University of Connecticut

ISBN 978-0-9997244-4-6

Response Speed, Neuro-psychological assessment, Persistence, Arousal Need, Association,Human Development

If a first grade chid and a twelfth grade child both score at the sixth grade level, no one can convince me that they arrived at that score in the same manner. To understand learning we need to look beneath these scores at the mental actions that produce them (Oscar Buros, 1978)

BLOOMER'S
Developmental
Neuropsychological
Assessments(DNA)

Introduction to the DNA series of Volumes

Developmental Neuropsychological Assessment

> *Until recently, ascribing a particular aspect of behavior to an unobservable mental process - such as selective attention-removed the problem from direct experimental analysis. The ability to locate mental functions to particular regions of the brain whose activities can be monitored allows even complex cognitive processes to be studied directly. (Eric Kandel, 1992.)*

Kandel's comment ushered in a new era for psychological assessment. The century old standby's comparing patients to the "norm" are fading. Instead of attempting to squeeze patients into in unruly categories, we have begun to explore the individual mental processes within the patient's nervous system. This evolving process assessment era provides the advantage of allowing the psychologist a reliable view of the specific mechanisms underlying behavior, and the further advantage that most of these mechanisms respond to specific treatments. I have chosen in the Bloomer's DNA assessments to deal with those variables which contribute to the neuro-cognitive processes involved in verbal learning and memory.

Why are we doing this?

Bloomer's Developmental Neuropsychological Assessments (DNA)is a series of mental or cognitive measures designed to probe the executive processes involved in Verbal Learning . It is a sequence of tools, designed to determine an individuals facility with significant neuro-cognitive executive processes essential to verbal learning and by inference most school type learning. The DNA battery of tests is a departure from the tests we are accustomed to, which tend to focus on declarative knowledge, such as vocabulary, or facts, or, tests that infer skill level with broad complex processes like reading comprehension.

The DNA tasks parse out known contaminants and systematically select, activate, and evaluate the efficiency of specific neural channels, to reveal the efficiency of simple neuro-cognitive executive process or operation. This approach allows the clinician flexibility, a much more specific diagnosis pattern, and allows development of focused treatment to remediate specific operations or knowledge.

Processing tests are not neural localization tests which point to effected parts of the neural anatomy. The DNA instead seeks to explore the efficiency with which the brain performs certain standard tasks. As such information from the DNA is of great value to anyone attempting to restore or build mental function, and to teachers, especially special education teachers, and rehabilitation therapists charged with improving the performance of children in academic type verbal tasks.

The DNA includes nine volumes. Each of the Nine volumes contains complete separate stand-alone instruments which may be chosen by the psychologist to probe specific executive processes. The Assessments are interrelated to give a complete picture of the client's neuro-cognitive executive functions for verbal learning. Each volume also provdes several independent probes of various aspects of the same general theme to provide a more complete picture of the breadth of the client's skills. The scores for these DNA assessments are sufficiently reliable to use for clinical decisions by themselves without resorting to compound or global scores and thus losing specificity of the assessment

A note in passing: I have been following this research thread for some 60 years now I have found the pursuit of neuropsychological assessment variables fascinating. I realize I have only begun to probe the great potential of executive processing assessment of human brain. I hope these explorations will stimulate more research and evolve into even deeper probes into the mysteries of processing inf the human brain.

Introduction
All learning rests on three basic executive processing skills:

1. Imitation:

2. Copying:

3. Multiple Discrimination:, the ability to reliably tell one stimulus from another and to act differentially to different stimuli.

Beyond these basics which normally begin to develop at birth or shortly thereafter and progress rapidly at first and gradually more slowly as the brain sheds or inhibits the myriad of possible alternate connections down, to an efficient few that allows us to stabilize behavior within our culture.

By the time a learner reaches school age we have usually determined that these three initial executive processes are in tact. The purpose of schooling is to develop, refine, and enhance a number of additional executive processes which allow the learner to approach and solve more and more complex problems. These processes are sequentially interdependent. That is, is takes a certain level of skill at a lower order component skill in order to recognize and attempt to learn the higher order process. This set of explorations executive functions is developmental, interdependent, and cumulative in the sense that one must achieve a certain level of mastery of one task before the next task can be successfully performed. For example, since stimuli in Short Term Memory fade relatively rapidly . One must achieve a certain level of response speed with the stimuli in order to maintain stimuli long enough to be acted upon. By the same token one must have an STM capacity of at least 3 units for learning simple letter/sound correspondences in reading; one for the visual letter, one for the auditory sound, and one for the process of putting them together.

 The DNA focuses sequentially on processes essential to verbal learning in a developmental sequence which reflects the interaction between processing skill and neural development. It is divided into nine volumes. The first eight volumes of the DNA explore eight different areas of cognitive processing.

The ninth volume, Sharpening up Old Tools" is wide ranging. It is largely reworking old tools, still in use originally from the early 20th century , to increase reliability and reduce error variance. For most of them I have been able to parse out some contaminants to give a clearer picture of the more subtle executive process.   There is considerably more potential knowledge about cognitive executive processes to be mined from the process approach. For many of these newer forms there are limited means, variances, or norms. For many of these revised forms there are limited means, variances, or norms. Over my long career the social barriers, particularly in the U.S. to empirical research, even such simple research, into human behavior have risen to such proportions that the time spent in meetings far exceeds the time spent in the laboratory. Being of limited forbearance, I have left the further research into these variables to those with more patience for social interaction than I.

The several volumes of the DNA are described as follows:

Volume 1. Individual Response Speed: The response speed to a stimulus class is largely dependent upon two factors. The first, the actual experience with the stimulus and the second the structure or the facility of the individual nervous system. The tasks in this volume index that basic speed of neural transmission. Once values for this basic level pf response speed is established, we then may parse out these individual differences in response speed, which allows us to uncover the variables of Persistence, Automaticitry, Arousal Need, and Purposeful Association.

Volume 2. Individual Short Term Memory (STM): STM acts as a gatekeeper to prevent the brain from being overwhelmed by stimulation. The five STM tasks are capacity measures. They provide indexes of the amount or number of stimuli which may be apprehended or acted upon at one time in auditory and visual sequential input channels and in written and verbal output channels . The Volume 2 tasks allow the comparison between input and output channel responding both with and without sequencing. Resting in part on the response speed of the nervous system, and upon the familiarity with the stimul,i STM is a limiting system to control the rate of stimulation that reaches the brain. STM is dependent in part upon the response speed. Since stimuli fade at a rapid rate, a certain minimal level of response speed is required to insert or maintain items in short term memory. Volume 2 also provides us reliable indices of a learner's Impulsivity and of Rehearsal Efficiency and Sequencing in Short Term Memory

Volume 3. Basic Reading Skills: The third requisite for progress within our education system is a set of skills and knowledge that comprise at least the bare minimum for independent reading. These include knowledge of the letters and phonemes in the language (a multiple discrimination task), the ability to blend these letter/sounds into understandable words, sufficient capacity to spell short words, and the ability to read those few frequent words that do not follow simple English phonetic patterns. The Reading Skills tasks allow the clinician to accurately determine each learner's missing knowledge, capacities and skills. This allows the pinpoint accuracy for development of specific plans for treatment of each individual learner and results in far superior reading skills.

Volumes 4,5,6. Memory:r Once the basic skills have developed the next concern is with long term storage or memory. These tasks represent the intersection between learning and memory.   There are two types of memory first described in 338 B.C. by Aristotle . Each type of learning has developed into a philosophical approach to learning and has it's strong adherents.

Volume 4. Natural memory (Association) develops without any necessary forethought or intention on the part of the learner to learn. It is the memory of animals in he wild. It's formation, largely pre-vocal, the result of vetting stimuli by the limbic system. Natural memory is primarily a product of interaction with stimuli in the world. The basic main mechanism is contiguity, the happenstance occurrence of stimuli in the same time and space serves to connect them. In addition to contiguity, stimuli tend to be associated by similarity on one or more dimensions. We use Word Association tasks to probe Natural Memory and extract a Free Spelling ratio, an Emotional ratio and a Long Word ratio to provide the clinician with further information.

Natural Memory, is often touted by the followers of Jean Jaques Rousseau 'Tabuila Rasa" philosophy. Many adherents to this form of learning feel strongly that it is natural, unfettered, and leads to creativity. On the other hand contiguity is most often uncontrolled, is often random, and more often leads to myth and superstition and cultural degradation. Natural memory happens whether you intend or not. It is fluid, disorganized and much more fun. Natural memory is introspective, responsive to the next stimulus in line, or to the physical/emotional condition of either the surround of the learner, and is often unreliable.

Artificial Memory In contrast, Artificial Memory is purposefully placing important events or in memory.   Without the stability afforded by of artificial memory human memory would be individual, personal, an sketchy. There would be no History of Mankind , nor any body of collective memories or procedures we could call a Culture. Our knowledge of Artificial Memory reaches back to the pre-historical times of Simonides who gave us a plan for remembering events and storing them for repetition. Since then many other schemes for enhancing the accuracy of recall have been developed. I have chosen to explore two of these Artificial memory enhancement procedures, Serial Learning and Paired Associate learning. Both are highly useful in verbal learning and both have considerable scientific background.

Volume 5. Artificial Memory (1) Serial learning, is the purposeful learning of sequences or ordering of stimuli or responses. These sequences aid in recall and allow one to perform tasks with less effort and more accuracy. While serial learning facilitates response chains necessary for efficient responding to more complex materials, the serial skill is the basis of most human complex operations and is a fundamental problem solving skill. The two serial learning tasks provide us with comparisons of Visual/Written with Auditory/Verbal learning , Acquisition Ratio, Seriation, Recall, Retention and Savings and learning set

Volume 6. Artificial Memory -(2): Paired Associate Learning. Paired Associate learning is forming a deliberate connection between two stimuli. Paired associate learning is the most effective procedure for learning factual materials, Arithmetic, foreign language Vocabulary, Science facts Foreign Language Vocabulary, or any factual material deemed worthy of long term retention. Using Paired Associate learning is much more organized, complete, and rapid, than natural methods.

Purposeful memory is often criticized because it is presumed to require more effort than Natural memory, however artificial memory is a skill in itself. Once developed a learner can become highly proficient. Artificial memory is responsive to systematic learning and repetition and becomes much easier as it is practiced. Artificial memory processes are important for organized stable information important enough to retain for any period of time. In addition practicing these procedures also reinforce the executive functions which make putting things in memory much more facile. The learner with limited skill in these Artificial learning/memory processes is a usually a poor student.

Volume 7 Complex Stimulus processes: Given the severe limitations in the amount of information that may be active in the human brain at any given time, a method of compounding information into simpler bundles is essential for manipulating large quantities of information. The most commonly used method is the development of conceptual hierarchies these are based on grouping stimuli based on a common feature. any items sharing this common feature are grouped into a higher order concept. This allows manipulation and storage of a larger number amount of information in a single instance. This compaction also involves a tremendous loss of information about specific stimuli. In Volume 5 we explore the learner's ability to approach concepts from several differing ways in a series of assessments that probe these higher order processes. Concept Formation, the ability to evolve concepts from exemplars, Concept Production, and Concept Synthesis the ability to evolve a new concept from features of separate stimuli,

Volume 8 Connotative Meaning, Limbic probes; we explore the operations of the amygdala, hippocampus and the limbic stimulus vetting system in this volume. All stimulatiopn must be inmitially processed by the pre-vocal limbic system which vets all stimulation for threat or reward value. We attempt to penetrate into the learner's awareness of the pre-vocal aspects of stimulus processing. We have developed new tools to assess the learner's awareness of word Familiarity, Active/Passive, Strong Weak; Sonic Affect, Emotional Ratio, and Imagery. These novel assessments contribute more than 20 % of the variance in such criterion measures as reading comprehension and probably deserve more attention than they currently draw.

Volume 9 Sharpening Up old Tools. A number of assessment tools in current use hark back a century or more. Many of these have marginal reliability or have the potential to provide us will additional inform lation   I have assumed the bravado of altering some of these instruments with a view of making them more useful or more stable. This volume includes several tasks dependent upon the perceptual and tracking abilities of the learner. Modified Gauthier's Bells test by enlarging the test to cover more of the visual field and changed it to increase reliability and to indicate the perceptual search sequence in more normal clients as well as retaining it's original

intent to assess hemianopia in stroke and brain damaged individuals We have Modified the Regard Five Point Test, Line Bisection, Trails, Tests A, and B Burtt Letter Maze, Stroop Test, Reverse Spelling to improve scoring and expose values for underlying executive functions.
test and a reverse spelling probe of the Reversal Shift

In summary, The DNA is a wide ranging set of neuo-cognitive assessment tools for in-depth probing an individual learner's executive processing . The DNA provides the clinician with an flexible tool which may be adjusted to meet each learners presenting symptoms. It provides highly reliable scores easily translatable into individual treatment plans focused on the specific process. We provide a method of approaching the poor learner which results in the identification of the specific processes which need treatment., The DNA is particularly useful for those processes used for the manipulation verbal type stimulation found in schools.   Application of the DNA to develop specific treatment plans, results in increased academic test scores and classroom performance.

Acknowledgments

This work is hardly mine alone. The science of learning and memory reaches back well beyond the recorded history of man. It rests on the work of many scholars and scientists reaching back into antiquity.

Donders, Galton, Ebbinghaus, Weber and Fechner, and Osterman, true exploreres of humam learning science are my immediate precursors. My own explorations of human learning have been marked by wonderful experiences. I was fortunate to have S.D.S. Sprague as a teacher in my first psychology class. He imprinted the scientific method on my young mind.

At Teachers College, Edward L. Thorndike and Irving Lorge shaped my scientific attitude. Robert S. Woodworth never let me forget that there is an "Organism" between the "Stimulus" and the "Response." Percival Symonds provided encouraging mentorship and laboratory space for my early experiments in human learning.

Much credit is due to Irving Lorge who selected me from hundreds of graduate students for his special gruff attention, and weekly thrust upon me, impossible tasks, one after another. One did not fail Dr. Lorge Irving. Lorge was my dragon, whose early demise has left a bewildering emptiness.

It was Nick Goldberg who opened the fascinating world of the nervous system and this work owes a great debt to his tutelage. His influence can be seen in throughout this whole series of volumes.

To my supportive partner, Jan Maya Schold, who gives me the space to think and create and an occasional jog to spur me on. Jan Maya. chipped in many of her precious hours to find and correct my many mistakes .

Within my personal experience. my grandfather Hermon Hutcheson pounded into my wandering pre-adolescent mind his mantra, "There ain't no such word as can't."

Last, and perhaps most important, was my own wicked step mother, Marguerite Barnes Bloomer, who with boundless patience first taught me "how" to learn. She also taught me, that "Learning is not fun." Learning is hard work; it is the accomplishment that is exhilarating, rewarding beyond all else..

BLOOMER'S
Developmental
Neuropsychological
Assessments (DNA)

Preface
These several volumes of unique DNA assessment tools set out to explore the neuro-cognitive processes that underlie human learning in schools and similar settings. For that reason they are limited primarily to language learning activities. The DNA assessments expose a deeper layer of cognitive processing than the usual intelligence, psychological, or academic type tests. They generate a more specific diagnostic pattern which allows the development of successful treatments specific to the cause of the learner's problem.

These DNA assessment tools have application in any instance where verbal learning is at question. Were we to explore other areas such as mathematics, or music, or athletics the form of these explorations might be very different.

A little history
My thinking about neuro-cognitive processes harks back to 1948 in a graduate class in experimental psychology taught by Robert S. Woodworth. Dr. Woodworth continually admonished us, 'There is an "Organism" in *between* the Stimulus and the Response.' To his way of thinking, important transitions and processes happen within the brain and nervous system induced by stimulation and affecting the very nature of the resulting response.

In that era psychologists were largely divided between the symbolic pseudo-scientific psychology of Sigmund Freud, and the more data driven Stimulus→Response theorists like Pavlov, Thorndike, Skinner, and Guthrie. Most of the S→R theorists tended to disregard these internal organismic changes. Professor Skinner dealt with the internal organism concern by simple stating that the inner world was just like the outside world, and thus psychologists need not be concerned with the organism. Although I became proficient with Mr. Skinner's Behaviorism there was always that niggling of Professor Woodworth's S→O→R theory in the background.

Let us think about Professor Woodworth "O," the Organism between the Stimulus and the Response. While what goes on inside the organism was totally confounding in 1950, Neuroscience now affords us the beginnings of an understanding. We knew then that if you repeated a response it became faster and more efficient. We have actually known that since ancient times, but now we know that this efficiency is caused by the neurons actually growing closer together and their nerve endings producing greater amounts of neuro-transmitters; so that learning and repetition eventually form a more efficient neural pathway or a network through the maze of neurons in the brain and body. During learning, in essence the brain establishes neuro-cognitive processes, or data processing subroutines, that direct, speed, or inhibit the learning. These neuro-cognitive processes are mostly independent of content, but put together in an appropriate order in the prefrontal cortex, allow for complex problem solving.

A second Impetus: Learning applied to Education
A second impetus for the development of these neuro-

cognitive process assessments came when I decided to devote my energies to helping children, by leaving the laboratory, and working directly in the field of education.

In the early 1960's I was tasked to teach a graduate course in Learning to educators. Having been trained in the science of learning I assumed that Verbal Learning was the basic science of Education. I anticipated that future teachers and school administrators would be somewhat knowledgeable and welcome learning even more of the scientific underpinnings of their craft.

The reality was quite different. By this time in the 1960's the science of learning had reached a point where, given a specific learning task, one could largely determine that there are several greater or lesser effective methods for teaching that task, and one could fit the method to the student and the circumstance.

My education students seemed completely unaware that there was a science of learning. For them, learning happened when you exposed children to stimulation. The more stimulation, the better the class. I discovered that educators were a faddish lot. At any given period there is only "One Way" to teach. In the early 1960s, that one way was "Class Discussion." Lecture was out. Reward was considered bribery. Workbooks were stultifying the child's creative instinct. Rote learning or memorization was anathema. Asking questions might embarrass or stress a student. Passive methods; Demonstration or Audio-Visual were OK, but only as a stimulus for Class Discussion. Children playing or fidgeting in class was OK because it was individual expression, and the child was not being coerced into following someone else's ideas.

Personally, I felt a good teacher should be a methodological virtuoso, proficient in a number of methods, and able to adapt method to each learner's circumstance. To foster this idea, and to expose my students to some ideas beyond their current educational fad, I developed a laboratory manual for that learning course, consisting of several modified classical psychological learning experiments. Each learning student was required to give this set of ten tasks to four persons of any age for four trials, to demonstrate different approaches to learning. Student responses to a laboratory manual in a graduate education course were widely varied. Several students complained bitterly to my Dean about burdensome homework. A good number just performed the task as just another step on the way to their degree. My reward came when an occasional student said "I never knew children could learn like that."

The benefit of all those laboratory manuals, to an nerdy scientific type like me, was they contained data! Admittedly, student assignments were more than somewhat specious, but I could not help myself from processing it into Means and Standard Deviations by grade, and found interesting developmental trends. These early student assignments eventually allowed me to refine these tasks into an highly reliable learning processes assessment tool.

Fortunately this was during the early times of Special Education law and schools were required to test children for special education. I mustered as many student helpers as I could, called in as many favors as possible and tested whole schools with what had by now become known as Bloomer Learning Test, or BLT. Over the course of a couple of years we were able to test more than three thousand children and adults with all or part of the learning tasks. I found the BLT test results made explaining *why* a child was having learning problems in school very easy, and prescribing appropriate steps to help him could be clearly defined.

The results were exciting. Each task showed developmental improvement over time until adulthood. Further each task showed a growth spurt at some time during pre-adolescence. These growth spurts seemed to occur in a sequence according to task type or complexity. Further, these spurts in task efficiency seemed to relate to children's typical developmental activities. Each of these growth spurts followed sequentially as though a certain skill level in the previous task was required to instigate growth the next. The tasks each related significantly to achievement test data and together predicted future academic achievement far better than the traditional IQ test. Further I explored the reliability of the tasks and found most of them high enough to use as an assessment tool for individual students.

Your brain, in particular your basal ganglia and your cerebellum, store a lot of processes, routines or methods of doing things. In general, your forebrain, the prefrontal cortex, tells you _when_ and _where_ to use each one. Neuro-psychologists are inclined to call these processes, directed by the frontal cortex, Executive Functions. I will use the term Neuro-Cognitive Processes because I am interested in determining _whether_, and _how well_, the learner performs these processes. As a Neuro-psychologist practicing in education, I, and my educator colleagues, are responsible for teaching efficient mental processes to our charges. I am much less interested in _when_ and _where_ our learners tend to perform or execute these functions than _whether_, and _how well_ they process information.

It is measuring the efficiency these data processing habits, or neuro-cognitive processes, which are reflected in the efficiency of a learner's scholarship, that are the subject of these several volumes of Developmental Neuropsychological Assessments, (DNA)

Over the next nearly fifty years the DNA has been used by psychologists in schools and clinics all over the U.S. and Canada. It has been revised and refined several times.

The DNA offers the clinician a unique view into the mental processing of an individual learner's. The resulting Developmental Neuropsychological Assessment, allows the neuro-psychologist sensitive empirical evidence of the learner's skill with dozens of neuro-cognitive processes and presents a unparalleled tool for treatment design and follow up. The DNA offers the clinician a unique view into the neuro-cognitive executive processing of an individual client's learning related mental processes.

RHB 2017

Bloomer's
    Developmental
        Neuropsychological
            Assessments (**DNA**)-

Volume I **Individual Response Speed**

Contents

BLOOMER'S

Developmental
Neuropsychological
Assessments (DNA)

Introduction toVolue 1- Response Speed-

Human Learning is no longer simply the presentation of stimuli and then tallying the responses as the old S→R rat learning theories would have it. S→R theory in it's time allowed for great advances in our knowledge of human learning, while brain science was in it's infancy. Recent advances in neuroscience allow us to probe more deeply into the underpinning processes of human learning. We now know the human brain, and animal brains too, do intervene in the learning process. In between the stimulus and the response there are a series of neural activations and cognitive processes which allow the brain to take raw incoming energy, make some kind of meaning, and redirect the nervous system to make an adequate response. In broad terms we are basing the DNA on an S→O→R theory where the 'O' is composed of a number of these neurocognitive executive processes that serve to modify the raw energy of stimulation into appropriate responses.

Bloomer's Developmental Neuropsychological Assessments (DNA) is a series of independent tasks designed to activate a specific neurocognitive process. These processes underlie learning in both children and adults.

Many learning problems result when the brain does not process information in a manner or sewquence to arrive at a satisfactory solution. The ability of the DNA to probe more deeply into human learning allows us to design specific treatments, or compensations, for inefficiency in a neuro-cognitive process focused on the specific individual deficient process.

Most neuro-cognitive executive processes improve with age and practice up to some individual terminal level. We present developmental scaling as a base from which to interpret, and to compare relative efficiency between neurocognitive processes

Volume 1: Assessing Basic Executive Learning Processes: Speed of Response

All stimulation goes through a sequence of neural processes to shape and instigate a response. These processes are routine procedures which the brain performs in order to manipulate or transform stimulation into appropriate responses. The efficiency of these processes underlies the effectiveness of an individual's learning. Bloomer's DNA probes these executive processes to determine the processing learner's skill to manipulate or change stimulus material to derive an appropriate response.

Bloomer's Developmental Neuropsychological Assessment (DNA) takes a unique approach to assessing the executive processes learners use to solve problems. Instead of measuring how much a learner has accomplished we measure "how" the learner learns. We probe the efficiency of specific underlying neural executive processes used in learning, memory and thinking. Instead of providing one, or a few all-embracing scores to compare the learner with his peers, we offer reliable measures of a large number of specific neuro-cognitive processes the learner uses to perform the acts of learning, thinking, and problem solving. We are interested in exploring the neurological processes which show us "how" a learner processes information to arrive at problem solutions

Response speed

Information, presented simultaneously to a group, will be reacted to in differing times due to a differential in the individual neural transmission This differential in neural transmission, or Response Speed is the subject of our first volume, Each learner's neural system reacts at a slightly differing rate of speed depending upon the structure of the nervous system and the quality of learning of the specific response. This rate varies among learners and represents a "Personal Equation" (Mescalyne 1795, Bessel 1803)

If information is presented at a rate of speed, or complexity, that exceeds that learner's capacity, the excess information is lost. Further, this excess information acts to inhibit retention and reaction to the whole stimulus milieu. This stimulus overload is not only disruptive to learning and retention, but the requirement to make an impossible response induces anxiety which is further inhibits the learner.

Response Speed varies widely among age cohorts. This is especially significant when teaching younger children. Our data shows individual differences in Response Speed for first graders may vary by a factor of three. This combination of stimulus overload and stimulus induced anxiety is most severe in a fixed rate school curriculum. These conflicts between an individual's Response Speed and the ongoing curriculum stimulus stream are responsible for most school failures. School aversive reactions are largely trhe learner's interaction with the "One Size Fits All" of popular commercial school curricula with their pressured rush to completion by years end

These neurocognitive executive processes involved in efficient learning do not leap full blown as "Diantha from the head of Zeus," but develop gradually over time from an interaction of the genetic neural structure and learning experiences. Bloomer's Developmental Neuropsychological Assessments generally follow a developmental maturational sequence from simpler elementary processes to more complex processes required for solving difficult problems.

Prior Assumptions
Volume 1 assumes the learner has developed some prior skills and knowledge. To succeed in the Volume One assessments the learner must be able to print legibly the letters of the English Alphabet and to write them from oral dictation. This requires at least rudimentary skill in the mental processes of Imitation, Copying, and Multiple Discrimination as well as some training in printing letters and short words. Most of these skills are encompassed in a good print script handwriting program like Professor Bloomer's No-Nonsense Handwriting Program. which provides a straightforward simple print script alphabet.

Volume 1 Response Speed
Volume 1. This first Volume deals with assessment of differences in cognitive Response Speed between individuals. Evidence from this volume affords modification of the rate of presentation of learning materials to more closely match the individual learner's speed of cognitive processing. Since speed, especially in timed tests, often overwhelms the action of more subtle processes, establishing the basic Response Speed for an individual learner will allow us to remove the effects of speed as a contaminant, using the method of Donders (1863) to uncover indices of Persistence, Automaticity, Arousal Need and Purposeful Association as well as removing the effects of Response Speed later in other complex scores later on in this series of assessmentrs.

Our interest in developing Bloomer's Developmental Neuropsychological Assessments is to single out, and reliably assess, the individual mental executive processes and to apply this information to increase effective learning and memory with specific application to learner's of school age

This is the first of some 9 volumes of assessments of the multiple executive processes related to school type verbal learning

RHB
Willimantic, CT June 2017

Acquiring Content without Process is empty learning

BLOOMER'S

Developmental **N**europsychological **A**ssessments (DNA)

Volume 1 Individual Response Speed

A BRIEF HISTORY OF RESPONSE SPEED

Response Speed infuses Psychological testing

Personal physical speed has been important in human affairs since prehistory, when the fastest hunter usually caught the prey. Speed has also been admired as a mental quality as well. For centuries—since long before intelligence tests were invented—the terms "quick" and "slow" were common synonyms for "smart" and "dull." In fact, the speed with which a child processes information is an important factor in determining how well she learns, and how efficiently she can complete school tasks. School curricula require learning progress in timed units. In a timed learning task, the individual's processing speed determines whether she is successful or not. The speed with which a learner responds underlies all assessments all higher-order cognitive processing.

The personal equation

One long-standing astronomical measure is the precise duration of the transit of a star across a hairline in a telescope, which represents the exact meridian of a given observatory. The traditional procedure was to

count strokes of a pendulum just before and just after the star crosses the meridian and then to compute the transit time of the star.
In 1795, Nevil Maskelyne, head of England's Greenwich Observatory, discharged an assistant whose measurements of star transits were always one-half second different from those of Maskelyne himself, which he naturally assumed to be correct.

Several years later, the German astronomer Friedrich Bessel decided to test astronomers against one-another. He found that no two agreed exactly with each other. The difference between skilled astronomers was generally less than a second, and this difference for each astronomer was relatively constant. His finding led to the development of a "personal equation" for each astronomer. Consider the cumulative effects of nearly one second difference in the response rate to stimulation across a whole learning year for a child in public school.

Response Speed and assessment tools

Time, and its companion, speed, are major factors in most human assessments. The individual speed for performing various tasks is often the overriding determinant of our estimate of the quality of an individual's performance. For example a timed reading test does not ask the question of whether, or how well, the learner can perform the components of the reading process, but on the hidden assumption that speed is synonymous with quality, a timed reading test asks how fast you can read. In essence speed is an undisclosed contaminant of in the measurement of reading quality.

Because most standardized psychological and educational tests are timed, Individual Response Speed heavily influences these global measures. The learner's scores are primarily an index of the learner's Response Speed compounded by the complexity of the neurological processes evoked. As a result, scores on these gross global variables provide little information about the underlying processes that contribute to the learner's level of functioning. Response Speed is so pervasive in part because it is simple and obvious to measure. It is one of the oldest psychological measures and is habitually seen as an integral part of most assessments. According to Woodworth (1938), who in turn drew upon the work of Sandford (1898) and Bowie (1913), the modern psychological concept of Response Speed has expanded from the field of astronomy in the eighteenth century. Over time there have been developed several psychological methods for exploring individual differences in the neurological transmission rate. Some of these require considerable time and equipment others are relatively simple.

Response Speed and testing

At the same time this emphasis on speed overwhelms many scores on most assessment tests. The Academic and Cognitive assessments almost always strictly time bound and depend not only upon the learner's ability to perform the task, but also on the ability to perform that task within a timed limit. A number of authors consider Response Speed to be the major variable in Intelligence testing (Eysenck, 1952, 1991; Jensen, 1980, 1982; Nettleback 2011; and Vernon, 1983, 1987,1990.) Most validity coefficients are really due, not so much to learning or ability of the learner to process information, but the consistent effects of Response Speed. In essence Response Speed can be seen as a major contaminant in testing.

This over-riding speed contaminant hides from us the more delicate essential cognitive processes which actually allow the learner to perform the task. Removing the effects of Response Speed gives a much more specific diagnostic screen, and provides information for adjustments to allow the learner to perform at his best.

While our speed variable predominates in nearly all psychological and educational assessments of human behavior, test scores rely not only on the speed of nervous transmission but also on the learner's skill with myriad underlying neural processes. While individual skills with specific neurocognitive processes contribute to a learner's speed, they remain hidden under the dominant speed factor. In Volume 1, we develop a reliable speed assessment that employs very limited neocortical processing, thus allowing us to parse speed from complex scores and to uncover the efficiency of these hidden more subtle neuro-cognitive processes.

In Volume 1, we parse out this speed factor so that we can look at the effectiveness of some underlying mental processes that contribute to the learner's performance. By parsing out the effects of Response Speed we are able to derive reliable indices of the hidden variables Persistence, Automaticity, Arousal Need, and Associative Efficiency.

WHY IS COGNITIVE PROCESSING SPEED IMPORTANT?

Response Speed in the classroom

If a group of third graders ran a race, no one would expect all of them to cross the finish line at the same time. Some run much faster than most of the others, and some considerably slower. In this situation, we readily acknowledge that each child has a unique set of skills, level of development, coordination, motivation, experiences, and muscle tone. Thus, it seems perfectly reasonable that children should run at different speeds. Nonetheless, the fact that one child is slower does not explain why.

It is less obvious that the speed of mental processing varies among individuals for many of the same reasons that physical prowess varies. If we were to ask the same group of third graders to read a page, or answer arithmetic problems, it is not necessarily that same child who wins each race. Response Speed is dependent upon the task and the neural circuit that is activated. Individual students would finish these tasks at different times, because their mental processing, too, proceeds at different rates. An individual's response depends upon many factors, but key among them is the efficiency of the individual's nervous system, which in turn reflects the individual's genetics, experiences, motivation, and anxiety.

 The DNA is designed to explore the learner's variations in Response Speed in that language system that tends to predominate school learning. Our Response Speed assessment shows the difference in processing speed between the slowest and the fastest child in an average age-grade class is a factor of three.

Response Speed in school learning

In schools, as in a large proportion of psychological and educational tests, quality of performance is determined by the number of answers per unit of time, in essence, Response Speed. School curriculums are designed to accomplish a given amount of learning in a year's time, in essence, Response Speed.   Thus, much of the correlation between the tests and the curriculum is spuriously related to the learner's Response Speed. The learner whose basic speed of responding does not match the time demands of the curriculum is ineffective as a learner and often develops a diagnosed pseudo-psychological disorder.

In practice, schools and particularly school curriculums tend to deny such differences among learners. School itself, progresses at a fairly constant rate of speed, depending largely on (1) the teacher's personal response rate and (2) the demands of the age/grade curricula, which are designed to move all children along at the same rate.

Children whose cognitive processing speed closely matches that of the teacher generally fare well in class. However, presenting learning material too fast or too slow may leave some learners out of the learning loop altogether.

As for the second, the standardization of curriculum materials by age and grade often does not provide sufficient flexibility for students who mature in Response Speed either more slowly or more rapidly. Curricula are sequential, requiring students to master last year's work in order to succeed in the current year. Failure to master the previous year's work nearly guarantees failure in the more complicated demands of a subsequent year's work. Many school problems are exacerbated because the curriculum proceeds at a steady rate that is different from that of each learner.

The rapid child and the slow child are out of synchrony with the happenings in the classroom. This asynchrony may have widespread effects on their behavior, their affective state, and their learning. Consequently, cognitive processing speed is a critical measure for the psychologist or neuro-psychologist working in schools, for it is often necessary to adjust speed requirements as a part of a treatment plan.

In many ways organization of our schools' all encompassing curriculum contradicts the educators stated concerns with individual differences.

Response Speed and Curriculum

Response Speed is a major factor in a student's success in school. As long as school administrators adhere to the mass production industrial model, with large schools, time- bound, lock-step, curriculum; there is limited flexibility for students who respond at rates different from the curriculum demands. Schools are organized around a curriculum which demands so much progress from everyone in a given period of time.

Teachers are often conflicted between the ever-marching curriculum, and the widely varying learning rates of their students. Many students are prevented from learning, not because they are incapable of learning, but because their Response Speed varies from the rate set by the curriculum. This curriculum induced failure is progressive and the disparity between the curriculum demands and the learners progressively increases as the curriculum marches inexorably toward its yearly culmination.

Since we assume the curriculum is written by "experts," if the child is not progressing at an appropriate it is a flaw in the child, not in the curriculum. One of the most common excuses I have heard from educators, for not changing a pupil's school routine, or pulling him out for treatment of some educational problem is:

"But, he's got to keep up with his class."

Countless students have gone without the treatment they need because of that "keep up with his friends" myth.

Further when a student is required to perform tasks which are not within the range of his Response Speed or abilities; stress, and avoidance are induced, making it even more difficult for the learner to focus upon his tasks. It is clear that the successful educator should be aware of the differential Response Speed of his charges and be prepared to alter the rate of presentation to fit the learner's present capabilities.

Our Measure of Response Speed
For Volume 1 we have chosen the simple method of the repetitive copying of an identical letter within a set period of time, Letter formation isa common school task, a simple physical motor response and is automatic in most individuals. It requires little or no cognitive processing and thus the task provides a relatively simple less contaminated measure of Response Speed useful to the psychologist and the teacher alike.

Our goal was to develop and standardize a reliable measure of Response Speed that was readily applicable by the neuro-psychologist in the office or in a school setting without requiring the use of complex equipment. We have chosen to use the number of identical single letter responses in a standard time period as a simple and stable measure of individual Response Speed. As you will see, our own evidence suggests that individuals vary widely in Response Speed, by as much as a factor of three in a single class. This basic difference in individual Response Speed, which underlies all cognition and all measurement thereof, has long dominated the construction of assessment tools.

Factors that affect Response Speed
A learner's Response Speed is affected by basic genetics, maturation, prior learning, and physical and emotional condition.

1. Genetics
Arousal and Response Speed are in large part structural, that is, genetic. The formation and efficiency of the neuronal structures are partially responsible for the rate by which stimulation may pass. Since stimulation must pass through an axon, the size and length of that axon are important determiners of Response Speed. Although many investigators—especially those who study reaction time (Vernon 1987; Jensen 1982)—believe that genetics can account for almost all of the variance in Response Speed, there are other considerations as well.

2. Maturation
The individual's state of development is related to Response Speed, for unless the nerves involved in the particular circuit have processed to the appropriate terminals, the Response Speed is slower. Furthermore, if excess or counterproductive neurons or synapses (ones that are not functional for the particular response) clutter

the nervous pathway, the rate of response is impeded. During the learning period while these neurons are pruned and responding stabilizes, Response Speed will increase. Thus, speed for most responses increases until the individual learning reaches maturity or automacity and is then speed slowly deterioriates throughout adulthood. Salthouse (1991a) estimates the effects of age alone on Response Speed to be an increase in reaction time of .01 milliseconds per year. This speed loss cumulates, so after a time, marked decreases in speed are evident with the aging process.

3. Skill learning

The history of the specific response has much to do with the speed of response. Proximity of synapses, neurotransmitter receptors and effectors, axon myelination, and a host of other neural features change as a function of their frequency of use in the striatum; all serve to control the rate of nervous transmission and hence the rate of response or the degree of automaticity. Developing automaticity is like building a railroad: it is an effective way of getting from one place to another, but it reduces the variety of paths and the number places you can easily go.

4. Physical and emotional condition

The momentary state of the organism—including general alertness, the recency of use of the particular nervous pathways, and the arousal of similar, different, or conflicting responses, also affects Response Speed. Priming is an example of a facilitation effect. If you think of the mind as an overstuffed attic, priming is like clearing a path to the place where particular responses are stored.

The general condition of the individual may also control the Response Speed. For example, the effects of physiological deficits of various kinds may be obvious or subtle. Many drugs reduce Response Speed, while others increase it; some differentially increase or decrease Response Speed and variability.

Most diseases influence Response Speed. Alzheimer's, Parkinson's, and multiple sclerosis are among the most studied, but others also affect Response Speed. Some of these—like HIV, headache, hay fever, alergies, and the common cold—affect Response Speed even during the incubation stage, even when the person is asymptomatic.

The results of the assessment tasks must be interpreted in terms of the neuro-cognitive processes they measure. Process assessments do not produce simple categorical diagnoses. Instead, deviant scores on process measures are signals that a therapeutic or rehabilitative program should be instituted, or that accommodations should be made for the processing deviation.

NEUROLOGY OF RESPONSE SPEED

Response Speed and neurological arousal interact. Response Speed is an implicit measure of the activation or arousal of the organism, as modulated by genetic and environmental factors. Without neurological activation, the organism is somnambulant or comatose. A sleeping, or unconscious organism has limited Response Speed. Effective learning depends upon a midrange of arousal—high enough to generate timely activation, but too low to generate a debilitating level of emotional arousal. Measures of Response Speed reflect the practical interaction of arousal with the environmental and genetic influences on the effectiveness of cognitive processes.

Personal neurological arousal is inversely related to the amount of stimulation required to generate a response. The greater the individual's arousal level, the more sensitive the individual is to stimulation, and the more receptive to stimuli the learner will be. There is, of course, an upper limit to this relationship, as in ADHD, or immaturity, in which additional arousal and stimulus sensitivity become debilitating, and the learner is unable to maintain focus

Basic to all physical and metal activity--including memory, learning, and thinking—is activation of the brain by the midbrain complex. One can view the midbrain as the source of the energy that drives the organism. In essence, the midbrain generates the neurotransmitters, activates endocrines and modulates the blood flow responsible for activating various areas of the cortex. Added to this degree of midbrain activation is the speed of transmission of the neurons themselves, which vary in both length and transmission facility. The degree of this activation controls the rate and complexity of both simple and higher-order neuro-cognitive operations. Measuring the learner's functional efficiency and ability to sustain this energizing system, and therefore the basic rate of information processing, is critical for planning educational or rehabilitation programs for the individual. The five Volume 1 tasks implicitly assess the efficiency of the midbrain, cranial nerves, cerebellum, and reticular activation system as expressed through the basal ganglia and the frontal motor planning.

Arousal is also genetically controlled. With maturational development and experience, including neural pruning, this basic rate of processing changes at differing rates for different individuals, usually becoming gradually both more facile and more limited in scope. The more practiced the response, the more rapid the Response Speed.

DNA Volume I
The DNA first Volume explores the individual learner's speed of responding, as an index of cognitive processing. The speed of the individuals neural transmission is critical to all learning. Obviously this Response Speed is critical in the performance of various timed learning tasks. Our index indicates the rate at which an individual can absorb information and effects the short term memory and the subsequent processing of information. Since most of our psychological and neurological assessments measure responses per unit of time, Response Speed is a major determinant in most test scores.

In a large proportion of psychological and educational tests, the performance level is determined by the number of answers per unit of time or limited allowable time per answer. At the same time this emphasis on speed or response time may overwhelm the contribution of the underlying executive processes we are trying to measure the individual uses to perform the task. In essence, Response Speed often overwhelms the intent academic tests.

Undifferentiated Response Speed, is the major factor in most validity coefficients. While Response Speed is an important variable in the design of assessment, teaching, and treatment programs, Response Speed also acts as a major contaminant which hides more delicate essential cognitive processes. As

Response Speed contributes to the major variance of an assessment it is more likely that the variable we are attempting to measure is hidden in the error variance and we have in fact hidden the very thing we are attempting to measure.

One of the goals of Volume 1 is to establish a Response Speed baseline for factoring out more subtle variables, so we may treat individual with varying differences in speed. As we explore the efficiency of underlying executive processes, this same Response Speed often becomes a contaminant which hides less dominant cognitive processes. To explore these more sensitive executive processes it is necessary to parse out the influence of response seed. We have used the procedure of Donders, (1863). This approach allows the neuro-psychologist to probe the mental processing much more deeply. These sensitive assessments allow us to focus on a learner's specific deficient processes in order to develop teaching or remedial or rehabilitation techniques. By compounding these executive process variables we are able to predict reading, spelling, and problem solving abilities far better than most time bound global tests.

DNA Volume 1 deals with five tasks (measures) that are related to a learner's Response Speed and are useful to the neuro-psychologist.

DNA Volume I Tasks
Our Volume 1 indices of the cognitive processing speed consist of five interrelated tasks that assess Response Speed. By using simple over-learned repetitive tasks, we rule out any higher-order cognitive processing to develop a basic neural speed index. In Volume I, we will assess each learner's Basic Response Speed

and then use this assessment to remove the effects of speed as a contaminant, and uncover better estimates the basic neuro-cognitive processes of Persistence, Automaticity, Arousal Need and Purposeful Association. The assessment tasks in this series provide practical diagnostic information related to student's work completion, homework, motivation, and arousal needs. The cognitive-processing speed tasks also provide important information about the learner's ability to maintain attention and to develop automaticity for verbal materials.

Bloomer's Developmental Neuropsychological Assessment Approach to Response Speed

Task 1
In DNA Volume 1, we measure Response Speed by the repetitive copying of single letters over a given unit of time. This test can be administered quickly and inexpensively, either in groups or individually, and with minimal classroom disruption. In addition, repetitive copying of letters and words is a close analog to common school tasks, such as handwriting practice and workbooks. Furthermore, by manipulating the stimulus and response requirements of repetitive copying, we will explore several cognitive processes in a manner similar to the Donders (1863) RT reaction time experiments.

Volume 1 has two major goals:

1. Measuring Response Speed
The first goal is to provide scaled score Response Speed measures in the traditional manner: to provide information about aspects of individual Response Speed to allow teachers, special educators, and rehabilitation therapists to modify rates of instruction so as to support a learner's optimum performance. Volume 1 develops five highly reliable, simple Response Speed tasks that require minimal neocortical processing. We present standard score indices of several aspects of the basic neurological Response Speed of the individual learner.

> **Activity** (Tasks 1&2) the number of repetitive letters copied in two minutes measures basic Response Speed, the rate at which the learner performs a simple, repetitive, non-cognitive task. Activity is an index of the neurological speed component in the individual's response. Activity has direct application in the adjusting rate of presentation of learning materials to individual learners.

2. Assessing Underlying Neurocognitive Excecutive Processes
The second goal is less conventional. Our highly reliable estimates of basic Response Speed allow us to add a small complication and then remove, or parse out basic Response Speed, according to the method of Donders (1863). The influence of speed thus removed, exposes the underlying neuro-cognitive executive process. Human information processing requires a wide variety of neuro-cognitive processes applied in given sequences. Assessments of these processes are usually obscured by the overarching speed factor. This procedure allows us to explore the brain and the processing that underlie speed-

related test scores. Parsing out Response Speed allows us to develop standard scores for numerous highly reliable cognitive-processing variables, which would otherwise be concealed by the speed variable.

By parsing out the influence of activity, we can obtain reliable indices of the following variables:

Persistence (Tasks 1&2) comparison of the differential rate for teo minutes of copying the first letter 'H' compared two minutes of copying the second letter 'N' estimates the likelihood that the learner will maintain Response Speed on a prolonged simple task. Persistence is an index of the learner's ability to sustain a level of responding. The likelihood that the learner will maintain Response Speed on a prolonged simple task, an index of the ability to persevere or withstand boredom of a simple repetitive task.

Automaticity (Task 3) the differential rate of copying letters grouped in a word compared with the simple repetitive copying estimates the learner's facility in merging letters into a word. Automaticity is an index of the learner's ability to group or chunk sequential responses for increased efficiency. Developing automaticity is essential for efficient learning and has direct implications for reading.

Arousal Need (Task 4) The learner's requirement for variations in stimulation, following six minutes of boring repetitive copying of identical stimuli. Arousal Need explores changes in the Response Speed where the letter to be copied varies randomly from one instance to the next. This differential estimates the learner's ease of, or need for, arousal built up from repetitive copying. Arousal Need, is an index of the learner's adaptation to variations in stimulation. This variable has implications for the learner's focus on learning materials and curriculum.

Associative Efficiency (Task 5) The learner is given a key connecting a specific number with a letter. Then the numbers are presented in random order and the learner's task is to write the associated letter under each number. The speed of correctly writing the letters estimates the learner's efficiency in making specific cognitive associations or connections between numbers and letters. Associate Efficiency is an index of the learner's ability to make an associative connection between contiguous stimuli. This variable has implications for factual learning, foreign languages, and science among others.

We may in siilar fashion remove Response Speed from any interesting variable and then scale it for instance
We can develop two supplementary measures based on the Wechsler coding subtest: the effect of parsing out the speed variable from these measures increases the reliability significantly and focuses the interpretation on the process of making associations between stimuli.

Coding ratio: A Score derived by removing our basic Response Speed measure from the Wechsler coding score provides estimates of the efficiency of associative connection between abstract figures and numbers.

Language/abstract ratio: A comparison of the Associative Index with the coding ratio measures the relative efficiency of processing language materials compared with the efficiency of processing abstract figures.

We will meet Response Speed removal several more times in this series of volumes where it is interesting to unearth a specific parameter bu removing the speed contaminant. By treating Response Speed as a confounding variable, rather than as a criterion variable, we have opened up a wide new variety of relatively unexplored, more subtle neurocognitive processes for exploration and treatment.

The simple repetitive Volume 1 tasks are designed to require minimal activation of the neocortex. These tasks are interdependent and should be administered sequentially within a single time period. The scores can be used directly to adjust teaching and rehabilitation therapies to match the abilities of the individual learner.

DNA Standard Scores

While The DNA provides standard scores for many of the variables these are not in any regard "national norms." National norms are of no value to a learner struggling to keep up with his class. These Norms are primarily a tool for administrators to compare their school against the nation. Our standard scores are designed to provide a base line against which to compare the learner against himself, and to indicate areas where the learner might profit from remediation or rehabilitation. These DNA bench mark standard scores are intended to provide the clinician with an individual baseline against which to plot treatments and to chart the learner's progress.

Administration of Response SpeedTasks

Total administration time (all five tasks) = 10-12 minutes

Note to examiner: The five cognitive processing speed tasks are interdependent and are designed to be administered sequentially, within a single block of time. Do not begin these tasks unless you have at least 12-15 minutes of uninterrupted, distraction-free time to complete all five tasks in sequence.

Equipment for all tasks: Answer sheet, pens or pencils, stopwatch

Volume 1 Task 1 Activity I
Directions

SAY: Turn to page 1. **(see page 80ff.)**

SAY: We are going to do a group of tasks to see how neatly and rapidly you print.

SAY: On the top of this page is the letter **H**, which you are to copy. You are to print your **H**'s exactly like this one.

SAY: On the next line is a row of boxes going across the page. When I say **Start,** print **H** as rapidly and neatly as you can, with one **H** in each box going across the page.

DO: Demonstrate the direction.

SAY: See how many rows you can fill in, in two minutes.

ASK: Are there any questions?

DO: If there are questions, repeat the instructions. Demonstrate if necessary.

Then SAY: Start.

OBSERVE: Watch the learner for exactly two minutes, noting your observations on the examiner's observation record form.

At the end of exactly two minutes,

SAY: Stop. Put your pencil(s) down.

CONTINUE immediately to **Task 2: Copying the letter N.**

See the Volume 1 Standard Score Worksheet for calculations of Activity scores. (Page 75 ff.)

Volume 1 Task 2 Persistence
Directions
> ***Note:*** *Administer this task **immediately** after the learner completes **Task 1: Copying the letter H.***

SAY: In the middle of this page is the letter **N,** which you are to copy. You are to print your **N**'s exactly like this one.

SAY: On the next line is a row of boxes going across the page. When I say **Start,** print **N** as rapidly and neatly as you can, with one **N** in each box going across the page.

DO: Demonstrate the direction.

SAY: See how many rows you can fill in, in two minutes.

SAY: Start.

OBSERVE: Watch the learner for exactly two minutes, noting your observations on the examiner's observation record form.

At the end of exactly two minutes,

SAY: Stop. Put your pencil(s) down.

Continue immediately to **Task 3: Copying the word HAT.**

*See the Volume 1 Standard Score Worksheet for the appropriate grade level for calculations of **persistence** standard scores.*

Volume1 Task 3 Automaticity

Directions
Note: Administer this task **immediately** after the learner completes **Task 2: Copying the letter N.**

SAY: Turn to the next page.

SAY: On the top of this page is the word **HAT,** which you are to copy. You are to print your **HAT**'s in each box exactly like this one.

SAY: On the next line is a row of boxes going across the page. When I say **Start**, print **HAT** as rapidly and neatly as you can, with one **HAT** in each box going across the page.

DO: Demonstrate the direction.

SAY: See how many rows you can fill in, in two minutes.

SAY: Start.

OBSERVE: Watch the learner for exactly two minutes, noting your observations on the examiner's observation record form.

At the end of exactly two minutes,

SAY: Stop. Put your pencil(s) down.

Continue Immediately to **Task 4. Copying variable letters**.

Volume 1 Task 4 Arousal Need
Directions

> **Note:** *Administer this task* **immediately** *after the learner completes* **Task 3: Copying the word HAT.**

SAY:　　　Now look at the next page.

SAY:　　　For this task, there are rows of double boxes. In each pair of boxes, the top box contains a letter and the box below it is empty. You are to copy the letter from the top box into the lower, empty box. Print each letter exactly like the one in the top box.

SAY:　　　When I say **Start,** print the letter from the top box into the lower box as rapidly and neatly as you can in each box going across the page.

DO: Demonstrate the direction.

SAY:　　　See how many rows you can fill in, in two minutes.

SAY:　　　Start.

OBSERVE: Watch the learner for exactly two minutes, noting your observations on the examiner's observation record form.

At the end of exactly two minutes,

SAY: Stop. Put your pencil(s) down.

Continue immediately to **Task 5: Associating letters and numbers.**

See the Volume 1 Standard Score Worksheet for calculations of Arousal Need scores.

Volume 1 Task 5 Associating Letters and Numbers
Directions

*Note: Administer this task **immediately** after the learner completes **Task 4: Copying variable letters.***

SAY: Turn to the next page.

SAY: On the top of this page is a row of double boxes. In each pair of boxes, the top box contains a number and the bottom box contains a letter. The numbers and the letters go together.

SAY: On the rest of the page are rows of double boxes with a number in each top box. You are to print the letter that goes with each number in the box below that number. Print your letters exactly like the ones in the top row.

SAY: When I say **Start,** print the correct letters in the lower boxes as rapidly and neatly as you can in each box going across the page.

DO: Demonstrate the direction.

SAY: See how many rows you can fill in, in two minutes.

SAY: Start.

OBSERVE: Watch the learner for exactly two minutes.

Note your observations on the examiner's observation record form.

At the end of exactly two minutes,

SAY: Stop. Put your pencil(s) down.

Interpretation of results

Task 1: ACTIVITY
Copying the letter **H** and the letter **N**

Response Speed is an index of the learner's base rate of individual cognitive processing. For most learners above first or second grade, this task is automatic and involves almost no cognitive processing. It measures simple Response Speed and is an index of the functioning of the reticular formation and the midbrain and in turn the fundamental cognitive processing of the individual.

The Response Speed of the individual may affect the length of time required to perform academic tasks and may also be related to task and work completion. Cognitive processing speed is also related to the rate of rehearsal, which may in turn be related to short-term memory capacity or working memory.

Reliability, error variance, and validity
The median reliability of the activity measure is r. = **.96** at the "truth" level. The error variance is 8%, and the maximum validity coefficient is r. = .92.

Application
The learner with a low activity score often has trouble keeping up with classmates and may have difficulty completing standard assignments or homework within an allotted time. This slower rate of response often complicates learning by interfering with rehearsal and short-term memory. Allowing the low-activity learner to complete work, either by extending time or by shortening assignments, is an important part of curriculum planning for that learner.

Cognitive processing speed is also important in social relationships, where slower expressive or receptive speed may impair social communication. The school Neuro-psychologist should be aware that slower Response Speed is often (though not always) a sign of low IQ, residual depression, or some disease affecting the brain. Further assessment in this area is recommended.

The learner with a high activity rate may complete work more rapidly and then require additional stimulation. Some learners may become bored and lethargic because of the "slow" pace of schoolwork; others may increase their activity and seek or generate stimulation, often in inappropriate ways. Some drugs—methylphenidate, caffeine, amphetamines, and cocaine, for example—may also temporarily heighten arousal.

Response Speed, as measured by the activity score, continues to increase by maturation and habituation throughout the school years, usually leveling off about eleventh grade. Although it may be affected by various factors—arousing stimulation, drugs, behavior modification, disorders such as depression, cerebral insult, or diseases like encephalitis—Response Speed is otherwise relatively stable through life. However, it gradually diminishes—at the rate of 0.1 millisecond per year—as individuals age.

Teacher nominations and the Response Speed
We had occasion to administer the Volume 1 tasks to volunteers in a small town rural school in Connecticut. 254 individual pupils from grade 3 to grade 8 were involved in the assessment. At the same time a teacher nomination schedule for a number of school related behaviors was filled out by each classroom teacher. The results of the teacher nominations were applied to the Volume 1 results. For each of the variables the teachers were asked to nominate the most likely students in their classes and the least likely.

The number of responses for each nomination in each category varied from 1 to 4 pupils the modal response being 2. The following represent areas where a significant, (or occasionally near significant) difference for the Volume 1 task was found. Since the number of nominations was unstructured, the degrees of freedom will vary from instance to instance. It is important to note that no significant differences were found on any Volume 1 task and nominations for behavior problems or disruptiveness in class. One might infer then that Volume 1 behavior is unrelated to socially appropriate behavior. Volume 1 tasks are however, related to a number of classroom activities.

The results of the teacher nominations were applied to the Volume 1 results. The following represent areas where a significant (or occasionally near significant) difference for the Volume 1 task was found. Since the number of nominations was unstructured, the degrees of freedom vary from instance to instance.

It is important to note that no significant differences were found on any Volume 1 task and nominations for behavior problems or disruptiveness in class. One might infer, then, that Volume 1 behavior is unrelated to socially inappropriate behavior. Volume 1 tasks, however, are related to a number of classroom activities.

Teacher nominations
Children who had significantly higher Response Speeds, as measured by the number of **H**'s written in two minutes, were more likely to be nominated by teachers as:

1. Working fast ($F = 3.84$, p. $= .05$ df $= 1/54$)

2. Being more active on the playground ($F = 16.7$, p. $= .000$, df $= 1/42$)

3. Learning easily ($F = 4.69$, p. $= .03$, df $= 1/53$)

4. Talking a lot ($F = 6.12$, p. $= .02$ df $= 1/45$)

5. Participating in class discussions ($F = 4.19$, p. $= .04$, df $= 1/46$)

6. Completing homework ($F = 8.87$, p. $= .004$, df $= 1/54$)

In short, children who were described as having positive traits for school success also produced a greater number of responses on the letter **H** task and letter N of Volume 1.

School-related problems
Since many conditions affect cognitive processing speed, this variable is significant for the school Neuro-psychologist. Speed of response has

been associated with a number of significant school-related problems. Individuals with retardation (Kail 1992; Brewer & Smith 1990), dyslexics with xxy chromosome (Salbenblatt & Robinson 1986), children with language disorders and reading problems (Bower, Steffy, & Swanson 1986)—all have slower Response Speeds. Aman and Mayhew (1980) found Response Speed highly correlated to the progress of remedial readers over a two-year period La Buda and DeFries (1988) found similar results over a four-year follow up, indicating some potential cumulative effects of reduced Response Speed. Children with behavior problems are likely to have slower Response Speed than children without such problems (Kupietz, Camp, & Weissman 1976).

Learning disabilities

We studied a sample of 143 individuals with learning disabilities in grades 3-6 from Connecticut public schools. Their mean scaled score for activity was S.S. = 09 at the 37th percentile. While as a group score this number is not statistically significant, individually we found 30% (almost twice the expected number of 16%) of learning disabled individuals with a scaled score less than S.S. = 07 (16th percentile). Thus, we conclude that limited Response Speed is more common in individuals who are adjudged learning disabled, but it is not a marker of a learning disability.

Attention Deficit Disorder

The picture for ADD and ADHD youngsters is less clear. Zentall, Zentall, and Barack (1978) reported faster speeds for hyperactive individuals, except on activities that required concentration. Sergeant and Van-der-Meere (1988) found that hyperactive learners were unable to use feedback to adjust Response Speed downward when the responses became more complex. The responses of medicated hyperactive learners were *slower* than those of either non-medicated hyperactive learners or normal children (Hefley & Gorman 1986). Barkley, Grodzinsky, and DuPaul (1992) concluded that a review of existing findings suggests a complex problem with perceptual-motor speed and processing in learners with ADD/ADHD.

Task 2: PERSISTENCE
Copying the letter **N**

Persistence measures the ability to sustain a simple, repetitive writing task—that is, an uninteresting task—for an extended period. It is an essential factor in maintaining attention.

To measure persistence, the second task requires learners to copy the letter **N** as neatly and rapidly as possible for two minutes, immediately after copying the letter **H** for two minutes. It is an extension of a Donders *a-reaction* task over time. We use the ratio of **N** to **H** without a decimal as our measure of persistence. The ratio of the numbers of responses measures the effects on Response Speed of continued repetitive action.

Copying single letters for four minutes is boring, and the rate of response begins to fall off. Persistence is inversely related to boredom with simple academic tasks. We use persistence and boredom as opposites in a bipolar variable. This measure is a behavioral representation of *boredom susceptibility*, which Zuckerman (1994, p. 32) defines as "an intolerance for repetitive experience of any kind."

Reliability, error variance, and validity
The median reliability of the persistence measure is r. = **.93** in the "truth" range. The error variance of this measure is 14%, and the maximum validity coefficient is r. = .86.

Application
In our study of 143 individuals with learning disabilities, we found the persistence variable to be normally distributed, with a mean of scaled score of SS = 10.0 and a standard deviation of 2.8, not significantly different from the standardization sample.

Low persistence scores often indicate a learner who cannot tolerate frustration well or cannot sustain a simple response, particularly in an academic setting. We may interpret this score as a measure of the learner's motivation to perform routine academic tasks.

Our clinical observations suggest that often this learner is easily bored, becomes easily overwhelmed as the assigned amount of work increases, and has difficulty completing the work. The learner often has negative feelings about academic tasks and therefore avoids schoolwork. Emotionally sensitive learners may attribute their own lack of persistence to consistent failure at simple spelling or word-analysis tasks. Low persistence is common in depressed learners or individuals with delinquent tendencies. Schools often see low persistence as a sign of immaturity or an attention problem.

A high persistence score indicates that the learner increases Response Speed as the repetitive activity is prolonged. A slightly high persistence score indicates a willingness to continue in boring, repetitive tasks longer than many classmates do. Slow learners often exhibit a mildly high persistence. High persistence scores may also indicate a warm-up effect. Extremely high scores may reflect perseveration or compulsive behavior.

Our clinical observations suggest that individuals who have low persistence and high impulsivity (Volume 6) also tend to have a history of behavior disorders. Often this combination includes an extreme deviant (either high or low) emotional ratio (Volume 9). However, high boredom or low persistence scores on the process assessment tests alone are **not** sufficient for a diagnosis of depression or any other disorder. They are indicator scores, which may be factored with other information to develop a diagnosis.

Task 3. AUTOMATICITY
Copying the word **HAT**

Automaticity is the optimum Response Speed for a specific stimulus. Its conceptual roots penetrate deep in the history of the psychology. Garcia-Sevilia, Quinones-Vidal, Vera-Fernandez, and Pedraja-Linares (1992) explore the relationship of current concepts of automaticity to William James's (1890) work on the differences between automatic and controlled processes:

> Man is born with a tendency to do more things than he has ready arrangements for in his nerve-centers. Most of the performances of animals are automatic. In him (humans) the number of them is so enormous that most of them must be the fruit of painful study. If practice did not make perfect, nor habit economize the expense of nervous and muscular energy, he would therefore be in a sorry plight (James 1890, vol. 2, p. 113).

The modern concept of automaticity is generally credited to Laberge and Samuels (1974). It refers to the ability "to perform a learned task quickly and accurately with little conscious effort or attention" (Naslund & Samuels 1992, p. 135). In education, rapid, stable, invariant responses are termed "automatic" (Laberge & Samuels1977; Samuels 1988).

The ability to group or integrate successive different responses into a single unit represents the degree of overlearning of the simpler responses. Copying the word **HAT** as neatly and rapidly as possible for two minutes immediately after copying the letters **H** and **N** Is a more complex Donders (1868) *a-reaction.* The task measures the change in rate of copying words as compared with the rate of copying letters. If the learner perceives the word as a unit, rather than as a sequence of unrelated letters, he usually copies more letters per minute. Familiarity with the symbols appears to affect the processing speed, according to Rudell and Hu (2000),

The DNA measure of automaticity, or response integration, is related to the level of automaticity of verbal learning. It may also related to the efficiency of the neural networks relating to learning to read and write.

Automaticity is a complex function of genetics, arousal, history of learning, and recency of practice. At the neuronal level, automaticity is a function of axon-dendrite synaptic proximity, neurotransmitter receptors, and myelination of the neural circuit involved in the response. Automaticity appears to activate primarily the subcortical regions. Using a radioactive dopamine precursor molecule and three-dimensional imaging to assess automatic responses to spatial stimuli, Nagano et al. (2000) showed high uptake in ventral and dorsal regions of the midbrain, amygdala, hippocampus, and medial prefrontal cortex, in addition to caudate nucleus and putamen, which correspond to the dopaminergic projections in the brain.

Automaticity of cognitive processes is essential for activation of higher-order learning processes; without automaticity, there is not enough cognitive space for complex responding. The child who lacks automatic letter/sound correspondences or number facts, for example, will certainly fail at reading comprehension or mathematics.

Reliability, Error Variance, and Validity
The median reliability of the automaticity measure is r_{tt} = **.94** in the "truth" range. The error variance of this measure is 12%, and the maximum validity coefficient is r. = .88.

Application
Automaticity is the result of overlearning a response until almost no mental energy is required to produce it. As learning becomes more stable, it becomes more rapid, largely because of changes in synapses. The relevant synaptic distance decreases, and the neurotransmitter receptors in the neural circuit increase. Automaticity reflects the language-related neural changes by measuring the increased response rate to letter stimuli that are integrated into a word.

The efficiency of a response depends directly upon the familiarity or regularity of association. For example, in a study by Greenham,

Stelmack, and Campbell, (2000), event-related potentials (ERP) were derived for superimposed picture-word pairs. In each pair, the meaning of the word and picture was (1) congruent, (2) semantically associated, or (3) incongruent. The researchers found differential ERPs under each condition. These effects affirm the independent processing of words and pictures and are consistent with automatic, controlled processing of words and pictures, respectively. It also suggests that the activation of one symbol system may be counterproductive for learning a second system.

Remember that automaticity is item-specific and must be assessed for each relevant stimulus. For example, even if a letter/sound correspondence is automatic for the letter **N,** correspondence for the letters **B** or **Q** may not necessarily be automatic. We will explore this concept further in Volume 5.

A low automaticity score indicates that the learner has difficulty integrating letters into words. In such a case, the psychologist's first concern should be that letter formation skills are not automatic. Poor automaticity may result from the learner's incapacity, from a teacher or a curriculum that does not afford enough practice and rehearsal for the learner to develop automatic responses, or from teacher boredom with repetitive practice. The psychologist should recommend additional training in either printing or letter recognition or both, if they are deficient. For the learner whose letter writing skills are automatic, the psychologist should seek to adjust the curriculum to fit the learner, rather than trying to force the learner to adapt to an ineffective curriculum.

Since complex responses are merely compounds of simpler responses, lack of automaticity in one or more of the simple components can severely hamper future learning. A lack of automaticity for elemental forms affects the learner's memory, because considerable cognitive energy must be devoted to perception of the letter and word forms. As a result, the number of items and the complexity of the processing that can be employed in working memory are reduced.

To ensure success in complex processes, it is necessary first to teach simpler responses until the learner achieves automaticity. The psychologist should always ensure automaticity of componential responses before assessing more-complex ones.

We do not generally consider an individual with a high automaticity score to be at a disadvantage that requires treatment or compensation in school learning situations. However, high automaticity may reflect extreme inflexibility.

Task 4. AROUSAL NEED
Copying variable letters

Arousal Need Task 4 requires the earner to copy variable letters, as neatly and rapidly as possible for two minutes, immediately after repetitive copying the letters **H** and **N** and the word **HAT**. It is a Donders *b-reaction* type task, in which the stimulus and the response both vary for each presentation, thereby requiring both stimulus discrimination and response choice.

Keep in mind that this task occurs immediately after six minutes of simple repetitive copying. Copying variable letters, then, measures a "release from inhibition" from repetitive copying and is related to the learner's need for change or variability in tasks. When compared with copying the letter **H,** which we use as a base rate, it measures the effects of increased stimulation, or the learner's need for arousal.

Most learners respond to the variable letter copying with an increase in Response Speed. In essence this change in rate of response reflects the individual's arousal need, or need for variable simulation. The learner's brain seeks a level of stimulation that maintains attention awareness and interest. The arousal level is in part habituated by the rate and intensity of stimulation.

Arousal need measures the individual's need for variability in stimulation. Whereas the prior tasks required repetitive action, in this task the learner must change with each successive response. The concept we are using here is Zuckerman's (1994, p. 31) *experience-seeking* factor: This factor [Arousal Need] seems to encompass seeking of novel sensations and experiences through the mind and senses.

Prolonged exposures to rapid stimulation, within limits, may force a level of adaptation. Overstimulation—exposure that exceeds these limits—may produce irritability or even seizures, which act as defensive shutdowns of the arousal systems. In contrast, understimulation can produce boredom and lethargy. Whenever possible, the learner adjusts his environment to control variation in stimulation to avoid either overstimulation or understimulation.

Reliability, error variance, and validity
The median reliability of the arousal need measure (r_{tt} = **.95**) in the "truth" range. The error variance of this measure is 10%, and the maximum validity coefficient is r. = .90.

Application
This Arousal Need factor is similar to the human need for stimulus variation, or optimal level of stimulation, demonstrated by Hebb (1953). Zuckerman (1979, 1990, 1991) has used the term *sensation seeking* to describe the high arousal need group of individuals. He has demonstrated four factors within general sensation seeking: thrill and adventure seeking, experience seeking, dis-inhibition, and boredom susceptibility.

Results of this measurement help us plan the direction and sequence of lessons for the learner. Farley (1981) has argued that arousal need is important in designing educational plans. High-arousal need learners would benefit from dynamic teachers and from variable stimulation within a flexible curriculum. Low-arousal need learners would be overwhelmed by such a level of stimulation; they need a more consistent, repetitive stimulus environment and a steady teacher.

Arousal need is reflected in the tolerance for stimulation or reinforcement. Individuals may adapt to a level of reinforcement or to a level of fear or anxiety and will perform to achieve their unique level of adaptation. Zuckerman (1991) cites considerable evidence that arousal need is related to "tough mindedness." Learners who have extremely high arousal needs may exceed the stimulation limits of the school, in which case they may seek stimulation apart from the normal curricular routines. Many of our media and video games, which are timed to a maximum exposure of 20 seconds per instance, develop high arousal need, which carries over into other situations, most notably school learning. For the high-arousal need learner, poor academic performance may result, particularly in situations requiring repetitive, rehearsal, or factual learning tasks.

According to Mayes (2000), arousal regulation describes the interaction between stimulation, stress, and cortical activity and performance complexity. Arousal regulation involves interactions among different neurochemical systems in the pontine and midbrain reticular formation. The balance of these interactive arousal systems serves two functions. First, these systems serve as gates that protect the cortex from excessive stimulation. Second, they facilitate coordination between attentional, executive, and sensory cortical systems. In a positron emission tomographic study, Kinomere, Larsson, Gulyas, and Roland (1996) showed activation of the midbrain reticular formation and of thalamic intralaminar nuclei when human participants went from a relaxed awake state to an attention-demanding reaction-time task. These results confirm the role of these areas of the brain and brainstem in arousal and vigilance.

Why do school Neuro-psychologists need to know this? These data suggest that a tangible reward may activate more of the brain than do abstract grades, stars, or spoken rewards. In education settings. As teachers, by the time we suggest tangible rewards for recalcitrant learners, we are usually collectively desperate. These data support the idea that tangibles, rather than serving as bribes, are a way of activating alternative sections of the brain.

Some learners produce more responses to variable stimulation when compared with a repetitive task. The increase in Response Speed when stimuli are varied indexes the learner's reaction to prolonged reduced stimulation and, conversely, the need for variable stimulation. High arousal need suggests that, when the learner is occupied with identical stimuli for a period, his attention begins to wander; he may drift off task as he adapts to the stimulation, which no longer activates the midbrain and reticular system. As a result, memorization and other simple information processes become annoying and less effective. The teacher or therapist may have to use short, repetitive lessons spaced over days. At extreme levels, learners with high arousal need may exhibit consistent inattention and increased alternative activity.

Other learners produce fewer responses to variable stimulation—perhaps as a function of lack of automaticity with letter forms, or insufficient arousal of academic tasks, or resistance to change or stimulus variation. At extreme levels, low arousal need may accompany rigidity, lack of flexibility, perseveration, or ideational persistence. Learners with low arousal need may have difficulty changing from one area or subject to another or may become agitated at a change in routine. For example, some children, after learning addition processes, have extreme difficulty with subtraction and continually regress to the addition processes.

A low arousal need may be related to complaisance or a desire to engage in routine or repetitive activities. Deviation from routines is often disturbing and must be met with careful adaptation. Low arousal need is related to depressive or obsessive-compulsive behavior (Miller & Marago 1977).

Birenbaum & Montag (1986) found sensation seeking to be highly related broad personality factor of *independence.* Baird (1981) found a similar factor —uniqueness— related to the sensation-seeking sub-scales. Arousal need is related to appreciation of humor. It reflects a disposition to seek stimulus uncertainty. Ruch (1988) found appreciation of humor related to sensation seeking, particularly experience seeking and boredom proneness.

Teacher nominations
Children who were described as "active on the playground" had significantly lower arousal need than those who were less active ($F = 6.67$, $p. = .01$, $df = 1/46$). Although none of the Volume 1 variables was significantly related to behavioral nominations, children with high arousal need approached significance ($F = 2.97$, $p. = .09$, $df = 1/39$) on the "disruptive in class" nomination.

Task 5: ASSOCIATION INDEX
Making connections between letters and numbers

The Association Index is a measure of the learner's skill at connecting two unrelated stimuli It is a basic process in education According to Jenkins et al.(1965), paired associate learning—analogous to purposeful, systematic, factual learning—may be viewed as having two components. One of these is learning the stimulus and the response terms. The effectiveness of this learning varies considerably in relation to the complexity of the stimulus and the response. The second component is the associative process—that is, the ability to establish the connection or relationship so that a given stimulus elicits a consistent, predictable response.

We have separated these two aspects to some degree by isolating the associative connection as a separate task from a conventional paired-associate learning task, to allow the clinician to pinpoint the learner's associative processing strengths and weaknesses.

The association index measures the ability to form novel connections between well-known automatic stimuli and responses, corrected for Response Speed. We remove the effects of Response Speed to get a pure estimate of paired associative processing by developing a ratio between the number of correct responses to task 5 (making associations) and the number of correct responses to task 1 (copying the letter **H**).

By using the ratio between this score and the score of task 1, we effectively remove the Response Speed and measure the "pure" associative processing between over-learned stimuli. The association index can be compared with the Volume 9 paired-associate learning score to determine the additional difficulty of stimulus learning. It can also be compared with the coding subtest from the WISC to compare the effects of a simple abstract response term.

The association index measures the efficiency of the processes for making deliberate associations between automatic numerical stimuli and letter responses as rapidly as possible for two minutes, immediately after the repetitive copying exercises and the variable letter task. The score is determined by the number of letters that can be matched with specified numbers in a two-minute period. In this task, the stimuli and the responses are well known, so no learning is required.

Reliability, error variance, and validity
The median reliability of the Association Index is r_{tt}. = **.89** in the "truth" range. The error variance of this measure is 21%, and the maximum validity coefficient is r. = .79.

Application
This task is important for isolating the cause of learning difficulties and for planning for pupils with learning problems.

The ability to develop specific associative connections becomes increasingly important in the upper grades, as school success requires more-factual knowledge and greater skill in developing paired associates. This requirement is especially evident in the learning of foreign languages.

High scores indicate a learner who is proficient in the process of paired associate learning. The high scorer generally performs better academically, with better reading, spelling, and math scores.

Low scorers generally have limited skills at making intentional associative connections. Such learners commonly have trouble learning factual materials in arithmetic, social studies or the sciences, or learning vocabulary in foreign languages. Since the association index measures the major processing element of paired associate learning, difficulties in the paired associate task or in factual learning may be related to motivation, to anxiety, or to learning the stimuli or responses themselves rather than to the associative process.

A low score on the association index may suggest a problem either with processing or with automaticity or short-term memory. The latter two should be treated, if possible, before attempting to deal with the processing problem.

Intentional association requires considerable energy. Students who are not accustomed to applying energy to learning tend to have major problems in remediation. Bright children who breeze through the early grades without applying energy to learning may struggle in higher grades, when classes increasingly require specific information.

Intentional association also requires considerable focus. Children with ADD who are not used to sustaining a focus often have difficulties with the association index, as well as with complex learning problems.

Association index
The ability of children to develop paired associates increases with grade level (Wiig, Secord, Jensen, & King 1991), as does the ability to learn strategies for paired associate learning (McGivern, Levin, Pressley, & Ghatala 1990). An effective paired associate processing is critical for retention in long term memory. Wang (1991) found that traditional measures of recall of paired associates suggested that older students displayed better

retention than did younger students, but when he controlled for differences in degree of learning, there was little difference. The amount retained, then, is determined predominately by the amount learned.

The inability to know and use strategies for learning, or even the lack of knowledge that learning can be intentional, is a major problem for students who are having difficulty in school. In our clinical practice, we often ask, "If your teacher gave you something to learn, and you were going to be tested tomorrow, what would you do?" The most common answer is "I don't know" or "I'd read it." Most referred students are not aware that they can intentionally learn something; so far, they have relied primarily upon incidental learning from television or listening in class.

The development of an associative learning strategy is important, because intentional learning requires facility with these strategies, and intentional learning is much superior for long term retention than incidental learning. Given the same number of exposures, incidental learning was about equivalent to the first trial of intentional learning (Crook, Larrabee, & Youngjohn 1993).

Teacher nominations
The association index measures a basic process in paired associate learning. Children who performed better on the association index were generally nominated as more likely to:

1. Complete their homework (association index: $F = 6.96$, $p. = .01$, $df = 1/53$)

2. Talk a lot ($F = 6.85$, $p. = .01$, $df = 1/53$)

3. Participate in class discussions ($F = 5.51$, $p. = .02$, $df = 1/46$)

Two other categories—working fast (F = 3.65, p. = .06, df = 1/54) and active on the playground (F = 3.95, p. = .054, df = 1/42)—showed higher, but not statistically significant, association indices.

Some additional data from the standardization sample indicated that students nominated as most likely to complete tasks or homework scored higher on the association index than did their peers who were nominated as unlikely to:

Complete tasks (F = 3.17, p. = .04 w/w df =2/151) or

Complete their homework (F = 5.42, p. = .005 w/w df = 2/142).

Optional: WISC CODING PROCESS

Coding RatioThe association index is similar to the Wechsler coding task, but with two major differences. First, the association index uses letters, whereas the Wechsler task uses abstract shape symbols, which are likely to be less automatic especially for young learners. Second, the score on the Wechsler task is confounded with Response Speed. If we remove the influence of Response Speed, we return an index of the ability of the learner to develop associative connections between these abstract shapes and numbers.

By developing this ratio, we have mitigated the effects of Response Speed in the coding task. Thus while coding itself correlates strongly with activity, (r. = .77), indicating the contribution of Response Speed in the coding score. However, when we remove Response Speed, the coding ratio correlates with activity at a much lower rate (r.= -.20).

This coding ratio cannot be interpreted as we would customarily interpret a coding or digit symbol score on a Wechsler test. A low coding ratio score suggests difficulty in making associations between numbers and simple abstract shapes. High scores indicate a facility in making this type of association.

Reliability, error variance, and validity
We have also affected the reliability of the task as well. The median reliability of coding for the WISC is r_{tt}. = .78 By developing a ratio to remove Response Speed factor, we also remove some error variance from the coding score, increasing the reliability to r_{tt}. =**.89.** Error variance = 21% and the maximun validity coefficient is r. = .79 We have developed a normalized standard score for more accurate interpretation of the coding ratio.

Note: This is applicable WISC coding form for eight years and older.

Teacher nominations
A low coding ratio is more prevalent in learners whom teachers nominate as being

More disruptive in class (f = 3.51 p. = .03
w/w 2 and 151 d.f.,).

As anticipated, the coding ratio correlates with the association index at a respectable level (r. =.72). It also suggests there is 50% of variance between these two scores is unaccounted for.

Calculations
Note: The **raw score** (the number of correct symbols) must be used to compute the coding ratio and the language/abstract ratio. **Do not use scaled scores.**

Optional: LANGUAGE/ABSTRACT RATIO

Language /Abstract ratio:The operational similarity between the DNA association index and Wechsler coding tasks allows us to scale a comparison ratio of the rates of processing with language symbols as opposed to processing abstract shape symbols. We have developed a ratio of these scores and have provided a normalized standard score for interpretation of the ratio.

See Volume 1 Standard Score Worksheet for calculations of language/abstract ratio.

The language/abstract ratio compares the relative efficiency of processing letters and abstract shapes in an associative connection task where the stimuli and the process are constant across tasks. Only the nature of the response term varies. The measure is sensitive to the subtle difference in the efficiency of processing language stimuli compared with the efficiency of processing abstract, non-language stimuli. It indicates the relative efficiency of the neural channels relating to visual language symbols as compared with those for processing abstract figures.

Reliability, error variance, and validity
The language/abstract ratio has a median reliability of r. = **.91.** Error variance is 17% and the maximum validity coefficient is r. = .83 Extreme scores are often found for individuals with learning disabilities.

Calculations
Note: The **raw score** (the number of correct symbols) must be used to compute the language/abstract ratio. **Do not use scaled scores for these computations.**

Application

The language/abstract ratio is designed so those with higher relative language abilities achieve higher scores than those are more spatially inclined who achieve lower scores.

Low scores on the language/abstract ratio reflect significantly better performance in processing abstract shapes than in processing letterforms. They suggest a relative difficulty in processing letterforms and may be reflected in the rate of learning visual language skills like reading and spelling. Clinically, low ratios are often found in individuals whose picture vocabulary is superior to their verbal IQ; they may indicate an individual whose talents lie in the visual arts or engineering. Such a score may also indicate somewhat greater difficulty learning verbal skills such as reading and spelling.

Teacher nominations

Our exploratory study of this variable with teacher nominations indicates differential responses between language symbols and abstract shapes in a number of areas.

Individual children who were nominated as disruptive, had behavior problems, talked a lot, and were easily frustrated tended to have significantly lower language/abstract ratios, indicating less language facility.

Those individuals who were nominated as likely to learn easily, complete tasks, or complete homework had significantly higher language/abstract ratios.

Our teacher nominations show those more inclined to respond to abstract symbols over language symbols are more likely to be nominated for:

"Completes Homework" (F = 5.07, P. = .028, df = 1/54)

"Stick to a task" (F = 3.68, p. = .06 df = 1/149) approaches significance.

While the high and low language/abstract individuals did not differ from each other in class disruption collectively, they were nominated for significantly more than the middle group who were not nominated for either:

Class disruption (F = 3.12, p. = .047, df = 2/151)

Admonitions about interpretations of percentages vs. percentiles

Each of the ratio scores above is multiplied by 100 to remove the decimal point from the significant numbers and to convert the ratios to percentages. While the use of percentages is sometimes a valuable way to communicate with clients, the examiner should exercise some caution.

The percentage that "A" is of "B" is rarely supposed to equal 100. To say that the association index of 44 indicates that associative connections are only 44% of the individual's rate of response might cause a client to conclude that this figure is bad, whereas it is actually about average.

If percentages are used, mean percentages should also be given to prevent misunderstandings. Otherwise, use standard scores and percentiles when reporting scores.

References
Volume 1 Response Speed

Aman, M.G., & Mayhew, J.M., (1980). Consistency of cognitive and motor performance measures over two years in reading retarded children. Perceptual and Motor Skills, 50(3, Pt 2), 1059-1065.

Anastasi, A. (A) (1983): "What do intelligence tests measure?" In S.B. Anderson & J.S. Hemlick (Eds.), On Educational Testing: Intelligence, Performance Standards, Test Anxiety, and Latent Traits, (pp. 5-28). San Francisco: CA: Jossey-Bass, Inc.

Baird,-John-G., (1981). The brighter side of deviance: Implications from a study of need for uniqueness and sensation-seeking. Psychological Reports, 49(3) 1007-1008.

Barkley, R.A., Grodzinsky, G., & DuPaul, G.J., (1992). Frontal lobe functions in attention deficit disorder with and without hyperactivity: A review and research report. Journal of Abnormal Child Psychology, 20 163-188.

Birenbaum, M., & Montag, I., (1986). On the location of the sensation seeking construct in the personality Volume. Multivariate Behavioral Research, 21(3) 357-373.

Bowie, W. (1913). Determination of time, longitude, latitude, and azmuth.

Bowie, W. (1937c). "List of articles and papers by Dr. William Bowie." Bull. Geod., 54(1), 172–188.

Brewer, N., & Smith, G.A., (1990) Processing speed and mental retardation: Deadline procedures indicate fixed and adjustable limitations. Memory and Cognition. 18(5) 443-450

Crook, T. H., Larrabee, G. J., & Youngjohn, J. R., (1993). Age and incidental recall for a simulated everyday memory task. Journal of Gerontology, 48(1) 45-47.

Donders, F.C., (1868, 1969) Over de snelheid van psychische processen. In W. G. Koster (Ed.) Attention and performance II, Acta Psychologia, 30 412-431.

Erdmann B & Dodge R (1898) Psychologische Untersuchung über das Lesen auf experimenteller Grundlage, Niemeyer: Halle.)

Eysenck, H.J. (1967). The biological basis of personality. Springfield, IL: Charles C. Thomas.

Eysenck, M. W., (1979) Anxiety, learning, and memory: A reconceptualization. Journal of Research in Personality; 13(4) 363-385.

Eysenck, M. W., (1985). Anxiety and cognitive-task performance. Personality and Individual Differences, 6(5) 579-586.

Eysenck, M. W.; & Calvo, M. G. (1992) Anxiety and performance: The processing efficiency theory. Cognition and Emotion; 6(6) 409-434

Eysenck, H.J. & Eysenck M.W. (1985).Personality and individual differences: A natural science approach. New York: Plenum Press.

Farley F. H., (1985) Psychobiology and Cognition: An Individual Differences Model. in J.Strelau, F. Farley, & A. Gale, Eds. The Psychological Basis of Personality and Behavior. Vol. 1. Washington DC: Hemisphere Publishing Corp.

Garcia-Sevilla, J., Quinones-Vidal, E., Vera-Ferrandiz, J. A., & Pedraja-Linares, M. J., (1990) La figura de William James como antecedente en el estudio del automatismo. / William James' figure as an antecedent in the study of automatism. Revista de Historia de la Psicologia. 11(3-4) 29-40

Greenham, S. L., Stelmack, R. M., & Campbell, K. B., (2000). Effects of attention and semantic relation on event-related potentials in a picture-word naming task. Biological psychology. 55(2) 79-104.

Guilford, J.P. (1939) General psychology. New York, NY: D. Van Nostrand Company, Inc

Hebb, D.O. (1955). Drives and the C. N. S.(conceptual nervous system). Psychological Review, 62, 243-254.

Hefley, R. D., Gorman, D. R., (1986) Psychomotor performance of medicated and non-medicated hyperactive emotionally handicapped children and normal children. American Corrective Therapy Journal; 40(4) 85-90.

James, W., (1890) The principles of Psychology. (2 vols.) New York: Henry Holt & Company.

Jenkins, J. J., Foss, D. J., & Odom, P. B., (1965) Associative mediation in paired-associate learning with multiple controls. Journal of Verbal Learning and Verbal Behavior, 4(2) 141-147.

Jensen, A. R., (1980). Bias in Mental Testing. Free Press, 1980

Jensen, A. R. (1982). Reaction time in psychometric g. In H. J. Eysenck (Ed.), A model for intelligence (94-132). Berlin: Springer-Verlag.

Kail, R., (1992). General slowing of information-processing by persons with mental retardation. American Journal on Mental Retardation, 97(3) 333-341.

Kinomura, S., Larsson, J., Gulyas, B., Roland, P. E., 1996. Activation by attention of the human reticular formation and thalamic intralaminar nuclei. Science 271 (5248), 512)

Kupietz, S. S., (1990). Sustained attention in normal and in reading-disabled youngsters with and without ADDH. Journal of Abnormal Child Psychology, 18(4) 357-372.

LaBerge, D. & Samuels, S. J., (1974). Toward a theory of automatic information processing in reading. Cognitive Psychology, 6(2) 293-323.

Laberge, D. & Samuels, S. J., (Eds). (1977). Basic processes in   reading: Perception and comprehension. Hillsdale, NJ: Lawrence Erlbaum.

LaBuda, M. C., DeFries, J. C., (1988). Cognitive abilities in children with reading disabilities and controls: A follow-up study. Journal of Learning Disabilities, 21(9) 562-566.

Mayes, L. C., (2000). A developmental perspective on the regulation of arousal states. Seminars-in-perinatology, 24(4) 267-79.

McGivern, J. E., Levin, J. R., Pressley, M. & Ghatala, E. S., (1990). A developmental study of memory monitoring and strategy selection. Contemporary Educational Psychology, 15(2) 103-115.

Miller, I., W., & Magaro, P. A., (1977). Toward a multivariate theory of personality styles: Measurement and reliability. Journal of Clinical Psychology, 33 460-466.

Nagano, A. S., Ito, K., Kato, T., Arahata, Y., Kachi, T., Hatano, K., Kawasumi, Y., Nakamura, A., Yamada, T., Abe, Y., & Ishigaki, T., (2000). Extrastriatal mean regional uptake of fluorine-18-FDOPA in the normal aged brain--an approach using MRI-aided spatial normalization. Neuroimage, 11(6 Pt 1) 760-6.

Naslund, J.C. & Samuels, S. J., (1992 Automatic access to word sounds and meaning in decoding written text. <u>Reading and Writing Quarterly: Overcoming Learning Difficulties;</u> 8(2) 135-156.

Nettelbeck, T. (2011). Basic processes of intelligence. In R. J. Sternberg & S. B. Kaufman (Eds.), Cambridge handbook of intelligence (pp. 373– 393). New York .

Ruch, W., (1988). Sensation seeking and the enjoyment of structure and content of humour: Stability of findings across four samples. <u>Personality and Individual Differences,</u> 9(5) 861-871.

Rudell, A. P., & Hua, J., (1997) The recognition potential, word event-related potentials to study perception. <u>J Exp Psychol Hum Percep Perform.</u> 23: 1170–1195.

Salbenblatt, J.A., Meyers, D., Bender, B.G., Puck, M.H., Robinson, A. Gross and fine motor development in males with 47,XXY and 47, XYY. Clin. Res. 1986;34:122A.

Samuels, S. J., (1988) Decoding and automaticity: Helping poor readers become automatic at word recognition. <u>Reading Teacher.</u> 41(8) 756-760.

Sanford, E.C. (1898). A course in experimental psychology, Part 1: Sensation and perception. London: Heath. Scheerer, E. (1984). Motor theories of cognitive .

Schmidgen, H., (2002) Of frogs and men: the origins of psychophysiological time experiments, 1850–1865 Endeavour 26,(4), 1, P. 142–148

Schraven, Thomas. 2004. The Hipp Chronoscope.. The Virtual Laboratory (ISSN 1866-4784).

Van der Meere, J., & Sergeant, J. (1988). Focused attention in pervasively hyperactive children. Journal of Abnormal Child Psychology, 16, 627–639.

Veldman, Donald J.; Peck, Robert F. Student-teacher characteristics from the pupils' viewpoint. Journal of Educational Psychology, Vol 54(6), Dec 1963, 346-355.V

Vernon P. A.,(1983) Speed of information processing and general intelligence. Intelligence. 7, 53-70.

Vernon, P. A., (1987.) Speed of Information Ptocessing and Intelligence. Norwood NJ, Ablex.

Vernon, P. A.(1990). The use of biological measures to estimate behavioral intelligence. Educational Psychologist, 25, 293–304

Wang, A. Y. (1991). Assessing developmental differences in retention. Journal of Experimental Child Psychology, 51(3) 348-363.

Wiig, E. H., Secord, W, Jensen, B. E., & King, C. R., (1991). Multiple perceptions of word relationships: Evidence of growth in elementary school children. Folia Phoniatrica, 43(1) 1-6.

Woodworth, R. S., (1938). Experimental Psychology. New York: Henry Holt & Company.

Wundt K. (1893). (Ed). Physiologische Psychologie Translated by Edward Bradford Titchener (1904)

Ysseldyke ., & Shinn, M.R. (1981)Psychoeducational evaluation in J.M. Kaufman and P.D. Calahan (eds.) Handbook of Special Education. (pp. 418-440) Englewood cliffs, NJ Prentice-Hall.

Zentall, S S., Zentall, T R., & Barack, R C.(1978), Distraction as a function of within-task stimulation for hyperactive and normal children. Journal of Learning Disabilities, 11(9) 540-548

Zuckerman, M., (1979) Sensation seeking: Beyond the optimum level of arousal. Hillsdale, NJ: Erlbaum.

Zuckerman, M. (1986). Sensation seeking and the endogenous deficit theory of drug abuse. National Institute on Drug Abuse Research Monograph Series. 74 59-70.

Zuckerman, M., (1989) Personality in the third dimension: A psychobiological approach. Personality and Individual Differences, 10, 391-418.

Zuckerman, M.,(1991). Psychobiology of Personality. Cambridge UK: Cambridge University Press.

Zuckerman, M. (1994). Behavioral Expressions and Biosocial Bases of Sensation Seeking. Cambridge UK: Cambridge University Press.

APPENDIX A

Volume 1

RESPONSE SPEED

RELIABILITIES,

STANDARD ERRORS OF MEASUREMENT

MINIMUM SIGNIFICANT DIFFERENCES

Appendix A
Reliability

Reliability is the most important assessment of the value of a test instrument. Reliability is considered an estimate of the amount of error in the test and thus whether a measure is actually measuring something. Without adequate reliabilities a measure is worthless and its validity evidence is meaningless. While Low reliabilities indicate questionable measurements, A high reliability is a guarantee that something is being measured. The much more slippery question of what is being measured is the subject for validity. In essence validity is dependent upon reliability. without adequate reliability any validity evidence is fraught with error and is essentially meaningless.

What is adequate reliability?

The magnitude of the acceptable reliability is related is related to the number of scores, or the population size required to draw valid inferences from a measurement. The smaller the population the higher the reliability must be. Thus to draw a valid inference for a single learner requires a much higher instrument reliability.

Individual Diagnosis: r_{tt}. = .90+

Adequate reliability is critical in the clinical setting where important diagnostic and treatment decisions about a single individual are made. Low reliabilities indicate a high probability of error in diagnosis and an increased probability of a faulty treatment plan. The generally accepted minimum reliability for an acceptable level of error for individual diagnosis and treatment design is r_{tt} = .90 or higher. Reliabilities of .90 and above are in the "Truth" range and are considered acceptable measures of Individual patients

Screening devices for classes $r_{tt.}$ = .80 -.89

For test instruments used to screen groups or classes up to about fifty for those who might possibly express some characteristic indicative of a diagnostic criterion, a reliability of r_{tt} = .80 or greater is considered adequate. Unfortunately, most instruments we use for individual diagnosis, particularly at the subdues level, achieve a reliabilities at the screening level, hence the information they provide is often misleading. Reliabilities in the range from $r_{tt.}$ = .80 to $r_{tt.}$ =.89, are in the "Casino Odds" range and interpretations on measures in this range for planning individual client's diagnosis or treatment is considered tenuous

Institutional Research instruments. $r_{tt.}$ = .70 - .79.

If the problem involves examining effects upon a while school or industrial plant a much more relaxed criterion for reliability is acceptable. Reliabilities above r_{tt} = .70 are considered adequate for this task. Instruments with reliabilities in the range from $r_{tt.}$ =.70 to $r_{tt.}$ = .79 provide no valid information on any individuals performance, skills, or abilities. To use information at this level is seriously questionable.

Population research instruments $r_{tt.}$ = .60 - .69

If the research questions involves large data sets, Americans school children compared with Japanese, or males compared with females, a much more liberal criterion for reliability Is acceptable. For Mass population studies with a data set exceeding 1000 or more a reliability of r_{tt} = .60 will provide enough stability to draw adequate inferences. Using instruments at this level for inferences about individuals, almost guarantees error.

Low reliabilities and ethics

There are reliabilities reported lower than .60 for some instruments. The use of tests or subtests with low reliabilities to explain individual behavior is not only fraught with error, but ir raises questions of the ethics of the clinician, reporting or interpreting scores of low reliability scores without serious caveat explaining the extreme probability of error.

DNA Reliability:

The DNA is designed specifically for the diagnosis and treatment of cognitive processing problems. Process Assessment instruments are designed so the unit of interpretation is the single subscale score. If we are to use these scores for treatment selection and design they must be accurate. High subtest reliability is critical to interpretative accuracy. In Process assessment the subtest reliabilities, should meet or approach the recommended r. = .90 necessary for stable interpretation of individual differences (Anastasi, 1983; Ysseldyke 1980; Guilford, 1939).

Since high reliabilities are critical for individual interpretation, most of the tasks on the DNAwere developed by administering a set of 40 to 80 items to a sample of 30 to 40 learner's and then selecting the subset that produced the highest Chronbach's Alpha using the SPSS Reliability program. These refined tasks were then presented to a second group and reliabilities again determined. Final reliabilities were determined by grade level, from the standardization sample itself.

The DNA grand median subtest reliability is r_{tt}. =.91. Sixty-one percent of the reliabilities reach or exceed the r_{tt}. =.90, the adequacy criterion set for developing individual treatment plans In addition 85% of the reliabilities are .85 and above.

Test- Retest Reliability:

With 'g' model testing, the test-retest reliability estimate, or stablility is usually considered the most important aspect of reliability. A high test-retest reliability estimate is an indication that the test is consistent and will produce similar scores when it is repeated. It is an estimate of the confidence the clinician can have in the test results over a period of time and thus the "truth" of the test score. While test-retest reliabilities are considered most important, in standardized testing they are often the lowest of the reliability estimates.

In process assessment we expect differing rates of change in the scores over time, Test-retest reliabilities are somewhat less important because the learner's cognitive processing is often in developmental flux. We expect change, and we are exploring flexible process, not seeking a stable "truth". We have primarily used Alpha reliability or KR21 both reliabilitiy methods insure that there is a sufficient range of scores to differentiate relialy when there is a change in the learner's abilities We expect test-retest reliability estimates to be quite low and variable during the learner's early school developmental years, and to stabilize and increase as the individual matures

We have used a procedure developed by Veldman (1967) to determine test retest reliability. The basic premise of this approach is that the in a standardization sample of similar individuals a test should factor similarly between successive years. Veldman devised a technique to estimate the similarity between factor scores which developed a score interpretable as the correlation between the tests over the year, or in essence a test retest reliability estimates. The test retest reliabilities for a sample of 958 learners from the standardization sample Separate factor analyses were conducted for each grade level and the factor matrices were treated by the Veldman et al.(1963) procedure The resulting reliability estimates are presented in table A-2 below:

Data from the standardization sample for the basic scores was factored
by grade level. The factor matrices at each level indicate the inter-
correlations between the variables. Reliability estimates are based on
the assumption that is test responses of children in the sample produce
consistency in factor matrices then the correlations between grades
would be similar to test-retest reliabilities taken one year apart These
data wererun by Herman Bates of the University of Connectecticut in a
program designed by N. Veldman to produce estimates of test-retest
reliabilities

Table A-2   TEST-RETEST RELIABILITY ESTIMATES
                BETWEEN GRADE LEVELS

VARIABLE   BETWEEN GRADE COMPARISON

GRADE 2/3	3/4	4/e5	5/6	6-7/8	7-10	11	MDN
ACT .76	.70	.77	.80	.95	.94	.87	.80
VSTM .75	.83	.87	.97	.98	.99	.93	.93
ASTM .97	.76	.89	.90	.99	.91	.87	.87
VAPP .95	.89	.86	.95	.84	.55	.90	.90

K-R 21 Reliabilities

Table A-1.R Volume 1

**RESPONSE SPEED -
RELIABILITIES**

	GRADE 1	GRADE 2	GRADE 3	GRADE 4	GRADE 5	GRADE 6	GRADE 7/8	GRADE 9/10	ADULT	MEDIAN
ACTIV-	.97	.95	.96	.95	.95	.95	.98	.96	.97	.96
PERSIST	.95	.91	.91	.91	.93	.93	.93	.93	.93	.93
AUTOMAT	.94	.94	.94	.94	.93	.93	.93	.95	.95	.94
AROUSAL	.96	.99	.95	.93	.95	.95	.95	.95	.95	.95
ASSOC	.89	.89	.89	.89	.89	.89	.89	.89	.89	.89
CODING	.89	.89	.89	.98	.89	.89	.89	.89	.89	.89
LANG ABSTR	.91	.91	.91	.91	.91	.91	.91	.91	.91	.91

Table A-1.-M.S.D.   Volume 1

RESPONSE SPEED
.05 LEVEL FOR STANDARD SCORES
MINIMUM SIGNIFICANT DIFFERENCE.

	GRADE 1	GRADE 2	GRADE 3	GRADE 4	GRADE 5	GRADE 6	GRADE 7/8	GRADE 9/10	ADULT	MEDIAN
ACTIV	1	1	1	1	1	1	1	1	1	1
PERSIST	1	2	2	2	2	2	2	2	2	2
AUTOMAT	2	2	2	2	2	2	2	1	1	2
AROUSAL	1	2	1	2	1	1	1	1	1	1
ASSOC	2	2	2	2	2	2	2	2	2	2
CODING	2	2	1	2	2	2	2	2	2	2
LANG	2	2	2	2	2	2	2	2	2	2
ABSTR										

Table 1. M.S.D.Volume 1

RESPONSE SPEED -
RAW SCORES

MINIMUM SIGNIFICANT DIFFERENCE

	GRADE 1	GRADE 2	GRADE 3	GRADE 4	GRADE 5	GRADE 6	GRADE 7/8	GRADE 9/10	ADULT	MEDIAN
ACTIV-	10	17	15	14	11	8	12	14	16	14
PERSIS	12	16	16	16	19	19	19	19	19	19
AUTOMA	9	9	9	9	16	16	16	12	12	12
AROUSA	16	19	16	18	20	20	20	20	20	20
ASSOC	12	12	12	12	12	12	12	12	12	12
CODING	10	10	10	10	10	10	10	10	10	10
LANGU ABSTR	15	15	15	15	15	15	15	15	15	15

APPENDIX B:

RESPONSE SPEED

RAW SCORE CONVERSION

TO

NORMALIZED STANDARD SCORES

Standard scores as Bench Marks

The DNA is not designed to compare a student against the nation or even against his or her classmates therefore the use of these standard scores differ somewhat from the usual standard score which attempts to scale the learner in regard to some national population. The standard scores of the DNA are to be seen as **bench marks** against which to compare the learner against himself In turn this indicates that all of the mental processes measures by the DNA are subject to improvement by means of proper teaching, or simple developmental maturation. A low score does not imply a deficient human being, but may idicate a different rate of developmental maturation or a paucity in teaching methodology. An initial score is thus a bench mark against which to measure progress of the learner's facility with a learning process. Scores are designed therefore to help the teacher emphasize particular areas of cognitive processing and to determine the efficacy of their methodology with a particular child

Development of the Normalized Standard Score Tables
Over 8000 individuals from ages 6 to 72 have participated in the standardization of the DNA. Over 1300 of these were cases referred for assessment of their cognitive processing. The standardization Data were collected from individual volunteers, classrooms, and referred individuals largely from Connecticut, Massachusetts, and Rhode Island, Other small amounts of data are included from Florida, Alaska, and Louisiana. The tasks were normed singly or in small groups, and hence the population for each task and each grade level vary. The 'N' for each sample is given in the standardization tables.

Children and Youth:

The DNA was normed by grade level from grade 1 through grade 10, rather than the more traditional age grouping. Usually the referral question has to do with the learners potential to perform in an academic setting. Learning task demands for learners are controlled by the teacher and by the curriculum materials which change by grade level, rather than the age of the child. The cognitive processing expectations of curricula seem to change from year to year and the child is required to conform to these expectations his or her age notwithstanding.

The examiner then will normally enter the table corresponding to the child's present level of schooling. Assessments performed over the summer months may use the tables for the grade level which the child is entering in the fall. The use of tables for grades the child is not currently in may be useful for decisions of retention or acceleration.

The rate of change of most learning tasks is diminished as the learner approaches his or her maximum capacity for that task. Thus, the standard score tables for grades 7 and 8 are combined as are those for grades 9 and 10 since there were no significant differences between performance at these grade levels. Where no significant differences in task performance was found between grades, the data were collapsed across grade levels.

Adults:

Standard Scores are included for Grade 11 through adult age 40. Our data show little change in any of the tasks from grade 11 until age 40. After age 40 there appears to be a mild decline in some of the processing tasks. There are few detectable changes in learning abilities after 11th grade through age 40, hence the standard score table for this adult group is all inclusive. Although the test is applicable for the elderly we have not yet developed a normative data base which explores the cognitive processing of groups over age 40, but a number of cases between 40 and 50 begin to show some declines. Use of the DNA above age 40 at this point will allow comparisons with this younger adult group, but not age level comparisons.

Sample Distribution

A limited sample distribution raises some interesting questions about the generalizability of the DNA Norms. Information processing is different from intelligence and achievement tests where the information tested is declarative and subject to regional and cultural differences. Processing testing is not dependent upon prior information, but upon how bits of information are moved and stored in the brain. It should be less influenced by prior knowledge or culture and more influenced by the ways information, regardless of the content, is processed. Methods of training, and level of development, are more significant in cognitive processing than the information processed. The distribution of cognitive processing across regions and cultures has not been sufficiently explored for us to deal with this question. Our speculation is that there are fewer regional and cultural differences with process assessment than

have been found with assessment of declarative knowledge.
We have not as yet, made attempts to develop a standardization
which is regionally and ethnically balanced. We have found the
instrument to be clinically useful with Afro-Americans, Hispanics and
native Americans as well as and the individuals we have assessed
from various regions of the country. These data are included in the
standardization sample. The instrument is currently being adapted
and standardized in Spanish in Caracas, Venezuela, and into
Mandarin Chinese in Shanghai, PRC.

Normalized Standard Scores. The notion of standard
scores as the ratio of the difference of a score from the mean
divided by the standard deviation rests upon the assumption
that the population scores on the variable in question form a
normal distribution. In reality thus assumption is not often
met. Further, we have developed a number of ratio scores
which, are by their nature "J" curves and clearly violate the
normality assumption. We have thus "normalized" all of the
standard scores found in the tables. This procedures is
accomplished by developing frequency tallies of each
variable and using the upper and lower percentile bounds to
provide the range of scores for each level of standard score.
This procedure compensated for each deviation of the score
distribution, from the normal distribution.

The normalized standard score tables include, in addition to,
information necessary to develop standard scores considerable
additional information necessary to informed use of each task score.

Definitions

Directly below the column of raw score ranges for standard score conversions are found the following bits of information:

1. "N" is the number of individuals upon which the conversion table for that task at that level is based. Since the tasks are independent and were not necessarily standardized together, and since grade levels where there is no significant difference are combined for the purpose of developing standard scores, this information is important to the user. In general the larger the sample the more likely the information is accurate.

2. "r_{tt}." Is the reliability, of the task at the grade level specified in the table. It is generally recommended that the reliability reach the .90 level before the examiner can use the test scores for individual program planning. Where the reliability is less than .90 the examiner should seek independent confirmatory data before using the information found in the table.

3. "C_{90}" If we set a reliability of .90 as signifying the amount of error we are willing to accept for a given score, it becomes clear that as the achieved reliability differs from the standard from of .90 we have a change in our confidence in the score. "C_{90}" is a measure of the confidence. It is developed from the ratio of the standard error of measurement for the reliability of .90 and the S.E.M. of the achieved reliability. It is converted into a percentage, and thus is interpreted as the percentage of confidence that the given score can be interpreted as though the reliability achieved the .90 level.

4.   "S.E.M." is the standard error of measurement for the scores, It is developed by the following formula:

$$S.E.M. = S.D. \sqrt{1-r_{tt.}}$$

In this case the standard errors of measurement have been developed for <u>raw scores</u>. The examiner should take care not to use these scores when computing the differences between standard scores.   The standard errors of measurement for <u>scaled scores</u> is found in the Appendix A - Reliability.

5.   "M.S.D." Is the minimum significant difference in raw score units required to achieve a .05 level of confidence. The M.S.D. is developed by the following formula:

$$M.S.D. = (1.96) \times (S.E.M).$$

Where the result is not a whole number the M.S.D. is rounded upward to the next highest whole number. This represents the minimum difference in raw scores for that variable which can be considered significant at the .05 level of confidence. M.S.D's. based upon raw scores should be used only for within variable pre and post comparisons.

6.   "MEAN" is the mean of the raw scores of the distribution used in the development of the standard scores and the reliability at the level in the table.

7.   "S.D." is the standard deviation of the distribution of raw scores used in the computation of the normalized standardized scores and the reliability at the level of the table.

8.   Standard Score Columns are found at the extreme left and right of each table.

9.   Raw Score Columns in each table are headed by the variable names and each row contains the range of raw scores which relate to each standard score.

10.   To calculate a standard score comparable to the raw score for a particular variable enter the table at the appropriate grade level and find the column header for the variable in question. Move down the column until the score range which includes the specific raw score is found. Move horizontally to the extreme left or right and find the scaled score corresponding to the raw score range in the variable column. record the scaled score in the appropriate position on the student record form.

Note: If the difference between the highest scaled score and the lowest scaled score in a Volume is '3' or less a general write up is permissible unless the clinician wishes to emphasize a particular score.
If the difference between any two scaled scores in a Volume is '4' or more, those scores, at least, should be treated separately.

Bloomer's

Developmental

Neuropsychological

Assessments (DNA)

Volume One

Assessing Basic Executive Learning
Processes

NORMALIZED STANDARD SCORES
TABLES

TABLE 1.1 GRADE 1 — Volume 1 — RESPONSE SPEED

Conversion of Raw Scores to Scaled Scores

Scaled Score	ACTIV	PERSIST	AUTOMA-TICITY	AROUSAL NEED	ASSOC INDEX	CODING RATIO	LANG/ABSTRCT	Scaled Score
1	>29	0-5	<(-25)	0-9	0-19	0-9	0-44	1
2	30-34	6-14	(-30)	11-24	20-29	10-24	45-71	2
3	35-38	15-34	(-29)	25-54	30-33	25-27	72-77	3
4	39-46	35-44	(-23)	55-61	34-40	28-30	78-82	4
5	47-52	45-51	(-18)	65-71	41-43	31-37	83-87	5
6	53-55	52-55	(-12)	72-79	44-46	38-40	88-91	6
7	56-65	56-72	(-4)	80-91	47-49	41-44	92-98	7
8	66-69	73-76	(-1)	92-102	50-52	45-47	99-101	8
9	70-76	77-82	0-3	103-110	53-55	48-51	102-107	9
10	77-87	83-90	4-7	111-121	56-59	52-54	108-112	10
11	88-94	91-99	8-11	122-126	60-64	55-58	113-117	11
12	95-102	100-106	12-20	127-132	65-68	59-63	118-126	12
13	103-115	107-120	21-26	133-152	69-79	64-70	127-136	13
14	116-120	121-131	27-38	153-159	80-85	71-77	137-140	14
15	121-129	132-155	39-46	160-186	86-92	78-88	141-161	15
16	130-139	156-162	47-63	187-226	93-103	89-96	162-175	16
17	140-147	163-177	64-65	227-275	104-128	97-105	176-199	17
18	148-160	178-205	66-69	276+	129-170	106-130	200-314	18
19	161+	206+	70+		171+	131+	315+	19
'N'	233	183	265	118	217	218	217	'N'
r_tt	.97	.95	.94	.96	.89	.89	.91	r_tt
C_90	1.83	1.43	1.32	1.56	.96	.96	1.05	C_90
S.E.M.	5.02	6.17	4.51	7.86	5.70	4.90	7.62	S.E.M.
M.S.D.	10	12	9	16	12	10	15	M.S.D.
MEAN	84.88	90.51	8.50	118.22	61.28	55.03	113.91	MEAN
S.D.	24.16	28.47	18.23	37.82	17.41	14.96	25.34	S.D.

Table 1.2 GRADE 2

Volume 1. RESPONSE SPEED
Conversion of Raw Scores to Scaled Scores

Scaled Score	ACTIV	PERSIST	AUTOMA-TICITY	AROUSAL NEED	ASSOC INDEX	CODING RATIO	LANG/ABSTRCT	Scaled Score
1	>33	0-9	<(-25)	0-9	0-19	0-9	0-44	1
2	34-39	10-23	(-30)	10-21	20-29	10-24	45-71	2
3	40-43	24-33	(-29)	22-39	30-33	25-27	72-77	3
4	44-49	34-54	(-23)	40-63	34-40	28-30	78-82	4
5	50-63	55-61	(-18)	64-77	41-43	31-37	83-87	5
6	64-66	62-66	(-12)	78-85	44-46	38-40	88-91	6
7	67-75	67-75	(-4)	86-92	47-49	41-44	79-98	7
8	76-86	76-81	(-1)	93-99	50-52	45-47	99-101	8
9	87-95	82-87	0-3	100-105	53-55	48-51	102-107	9
10	96-105	88-95	4-7	106-115	56-59	49-54	103-112	10
11	106-113	96-101	8-11	116-123	60-64	55-58	113-117	11
12	114-123	102-110	12-20	124-141	65-68	59-63	118-126	12
13	124-140	111-124	21-26	142-184	69-79	64-70	127-136	13
14	141-148	125-132	27-38	185-208	80-85	71-77	137-140	14
15	149-161	133-146	39-46	209-272	86-92	78-88	141-161	15
16	162-178	147-165	47-63	273-473	93-103	89-96	162-175	16
17	179-245	166-202	64-65	474-612	104-128	97-105	176-199	17
18	264-290	203-255	66-69	613+	129-170	106-130	200-314	18
19	291+	256+	70+		171+	131+	315+	19
'N'	304	956	265	199	217	218	217	'N'
r_{tt}	.95	.91	.94	.99	.89	.89	.91	r_{tt}
C_{90}	1.43	1.05	1.32	3.16	.96	.96	1.05	C_{90}
S.E.M.	8.47	7.84	4.51	9.71	5.70	4.90	7.62	S.E.M.
M.S.D.	17	16	9	19	12	10	15	M.S.D.
MEAN	103.90	94.23	8.50	130.64	61.28	55.03	113.91	MEAN
S.D.	36.23	26.80	18.23	78.27	17.41	14.96	25.34	S.D.

Table 1.3   GRADE 3   Volume 1   RESPONSE SPEED

Conversion of Raw Scores to Scaled Scores

Scaled Score	ACTIV	PERSIST	AUTOMA-TICITY	AROUSAL NEED	ASSOC INDEX	CODING RATIO	LANG/ABSTRCT	Scaled Score
1	>31	0-9	<(-99)	0-14	0-19	0-9	0-44	1
2	32-44	10-23	(-63)	15-35	20-29	10-24	45-71	2
3	45-57	24-33	(-38)	36-55	30-33	25-27	72-77	3
4	58-67	34-54	(-13)	56-71	34-40	28-30	78-82	4
5	68-78	55-61	(-9)	72-81	41-43	31-37	83-87	5
6	79-83	62-66	(-4)	82-85	44-46	38-40	88-91	6
7	84-92	67-75	(-3)-2	86-95	47-49	41-44	79-98	7
8	93-101	76-81	3-7	96-99	50-52	45-47	99-101	8
9	102-113	82-87	8-13	100-108	53-55	48-51	102-107	9
10	114-122	88-95	14-21	109-115	56-59	49-54	108-112	10
11	123-137	96-101	22-25	116-126	60-64	55-58	113-117	11
12	138-152	102-110	26-34	127-138	65-68	59-63	118-126	12
13	153-177	111-124	35-46	139-150	69-79	64-70	127-136	13
14	178-194	125-132	47-56	151-165	80-85	71-77	137-140	14
15	195-218	133-146	57-65	166-187	86-92	78-88	141-161	15
16	219-232	147-165	66-78	188-220	93-103	89-96	162-175	16
17	233-263	166-202	79-91	221-245	104-128	97-105	176-199	17
18	264-304	203-255	92-145	246-324	129-170	106-130	200-314	18
19	305+	256+	146+	325+	171+	131+	315+	19
'N'	304	956	265	176	217	218	217	'N'
r_{tt}	.96	.91	.94	.95	.89	.89	.91	r_{tt}
C_{90}	1.56	1.05	1.32	1.43	.96	.96	1.05	C_{90}
S.E.M.	7.70	7.84	4.51	8.10	5.70	4.90	7.62	S.E.M.
M.S.D.	15	16	9	16	12	10	15	M.S.D.
MEAN	103.90	94.23	8.50	119.33	61.28	55.03	113.91	MEAN
S.D.	36.23	26.80	18.23	35.58	17.41	14.96	25.34	S.D.

Table 1.4   GRADE 4

Volume 1.   RESPONSE SPEED
Conversion of Raw Scores to Scaled Scores

Scaled Score	ACTIV	PERSIST	AUTOMA-TICITY	AROUSAL NEED	ASSOC INDEX	CODING RATIO	LANG/ABSTRCT	Scaled Score
1	>26	0-9	<(-99)	0-12	0-19	0-9	0-44	1
2	27-40	10-23	(-63)	13-31	20-29	10-24	45-71	2
3	41-69	24-33	(-38)	32-43	30-33	25-27	72-77	3
4	70-76	34-54	(-13)	44-74	34-40	28-30	78-82	4
5	77-91	55-61	(-9)	75-80	41-43	31-37	83-87	5
6	92-98	62-66	(-4)	81-87	44-46	38-40	88-91	6
7	99-109	67-75	(-3)-2	88-96	47-49	41-44	79-98	7
8	110-123	76-81	3-7	97-105	50-52	45-47	99-101	8
9	124-134	82-87	8-13	106-112	53-55	48-51	102-107	9
10	135-143	88-95	14-21	113-117	56-59	49-54	108-112	10
11	144-154	96-101	22-25	118-124	60-64	55-58	113-117	11
12	155-163	102-110	26-34	125-130	65-68	59-63	118-126	12
13	164-178	111-124	35-46	131-139	69-79	64-70	127-136	13
14	179-186	125-132	47-56	140-145	80-85	71-77	137-140	14
15	187-201	133-146	57-65	146-173	86-92	78-88	141-161	15
16	202-208	147-165	66-78	174-190	93-103	89-96	162-175	16
17	209-234	166-202	79-91	191-204	104-128	97-105	176-199	17
18	235-255	203-255	92-145	205-445	129-170	106-130	200-314	18
19	256+	256+	146+	446+	171+	131+	315+	19
'N'	304	956	265	207	217	218	217	'N'
r_{tt}	.95	.91	.94	.93	.89	.89	.91	r_{tt}
C_{90}	1.43	1.05	1.32	1.19	.96	.96	1.05	C_{90}
S.E.M.	7.03	7.84	4.51	9.01	5.70	4.90	7.62	S.E.M.
M.S.D.	14	16	9	18	12	10	15	M.S.D.
MEAN	139.33	94.23	8.50	116.33	61.28	55.03	113.91	MEAN
S.D.	33.69	26.80	18.23	34.53	17.41	14.96	25.34	S.D

Table 1.4   GRADE   5

Volume 1. RESPONSE SPEED
Conversion of Raw Scores to Scaled Scores

Scaled Score	ACTIV	PERSIST	AUTOMA-TICITY	AROUSAL NEED	ASSOC INDEX	CODING RATIO	LANG/ABSTRCT	Scaled Score
1	>53	0-8	<(-97)	-0-	0-19	0-9	0-44	1
2	54-61	9-36	(-96)	1-11	20-29	10-24	45-71	2
3	62-81	37-47	(-46)	12-56	30-33	25-27	72-77	3
4	82-95	48-63	(-16)	57-73	34-40	28-30	78-82	4
5	96-103	64-70	(-9)	74-81	41-43	31-37	83-87	5
6	104-110	71-74	(-8)-1	82-88	44-46	38-40	88-91	6
7	111-119	75-82	2-10	89-97	47-49	41-44	92-98	7
8	120-129	83-87	11-16	98-104	50-52	45-47	99-101	8
9	130-139	88-93	17-23	105-112	53-55	48-51	102-107	9
10	140-150	94-99	24-33	113-119	56-59	49-54	108-112	10
11	151-158	100-104	34-39	120-126	60-64	55-58	113-117	11
12	159-168	105-111	40-50	127-136	65-68	59-63	118-126	12
13	169-186	112-121	51-63	137-147	69-79	64-70	127-136	13
14	187-191	122-128	64-72	148-159	80-85	71-77	137-140	14
15	192-203	129-142	73-91	160-179	86-92	78-88	141-161	15
16	204-219	143-164	92-114	180-199	93-103	89-96	162-175	16
17	220-244	165-202	115-161	200-241	104-128	97-105	176-199	17
18	245-252	203-355	162-198	242-356	129-170	106-130	200-314	18
19	253+	356+	199+	357+	171+	131+	315+	19
'N'	292	1147	699	499	217	218	217	'N'
r_{tt}	.95	.93	.93	.95	.89	.89	.91	r_{tt}
C_{90}	1.43	1.19	1.19	1.43	.96	.96	1.05	C_{90}
S.E.M.	5.82	9.32	8.31	10.09	5.70	4.90	7.62	S.E.M.
M.S.D.	11	19	16	20	12	10	15	M.S.D.
MEAN	146.46	99.01	31.33	119.96	61.28	55.03	113.91	MEAN
S.D.	31.63	34.50	31.62	46.33	17.41	14.96	25.34	S.D.

Table 1.6   GRADE 6

Volume 4. RESPONSE SPEED
Conversion of Raw Scores to Scaled Scores

Scaled Score	ACTIV	PERSIST	AUTOMA-TICITY	AROUSAL NEED	ASSOC INDEX	CODING RATIO	LANG/AESTRCT	Scaled Score
1	>74	0-8	<(-97)	-0-	0-19	0-9	0-44	1
2	75-78	9-36	(-96)	1-11	20-29	10-24	45-71	2
3	79-108	37-47	(-46)	12-56	30-33	25-27	72-77	3
4	109-118	48-63	(-16)	57-73	34-40	28-30	78-82	4
5	119-128	64-70	(-9)	74-81	41-43	31-37	83-87	5
6	129-139	71-74	(-8)-1	82-88	44-46	38-40	88-91	6
7	140-150	75-82	2-10	89-97	47-49	41-44	93-98	7
8	151-158	83-87	11-16	98-104	50-52	45-47	95-101	8
9	159-166	88-93	17-23	105-112	53-55	48-51	102-107	9
10	167-176	94-99	24-33	113-119	56-59	49-54	108-112	10
11	177-190	100-104	34-39	120-126	60-64	55-58	113-117	11
12	191-201	105-111	40-50	127-136	65-68	59-63	118-126	12
13	202-218	112-121	51-63	137-147	69-79	64-70	127-136	13
14	219-226	122-128	64-72	148-159	80-85	71-77	137-140	14
15	227-238	129-142	73-91	160-179	86-92	78-88	141-161	15
16	239-248	143-164	92-114	180-199	93-103	89-96	162-175	16
17	249-259	165-202	115-161	200-241	104-128	97-105	176-199	17
18	260-275	203-355	162-198	242-356	129-170	106-130	200-314	18
19	276+	356+	199+	357+	171+	131+	315+	19
'N'	284	1147	699	499	217	218	217	'N'
r_{tt}	.95	.93	.93	.95	.89	.89	.91	r_{tt}
C_{90}	1.43	1.19	1.19	1.43	.96	.96	1.05	C_{90}
S.E.M.	3.94	9.32	8.31	10.09	5.70	4.90	7.62	S.E.M.
M.S.D.	8	19	16	20	12	10	15	M.S.D.
MEAN	175.99	99.01	31.33	119.96	61.28	55.03	113.91	MEAN
S.D.	33.63	34.50	31.62	46.33	17.41	14.96	25.34	S.D.

Table 1.7-8   GRADES 7-8   Volume 1 RESPONSE SPEED
Conversion of Raw Scores to Scaled Scores

Scaled Score	ACTIV	PERSIST	AUTOMA-TICITY	AROUSAL NEED	ASSOC INDEX	CODING RATIO	LANG/ABSTRCT	Scaled Score
1	>52	0-8	<(-97)	-0-	0-19	0-9	0-44	1
2	53-58	9-36	(-96)	1-11	20-29	10-24	45-71	2
3	59-68	37-47	(-46)	12-56	30-33	25-27	72-77	3
4	69-97	48-63	(-16)	57-73	34-40	28-30	78-82	4
5	98-124	64-70	(-9)	74-81	41-43	31-37	83-87	5
6	125-134	71-74	(-8)-1	82-88	44-46	38-40	88-91	6
7	135-152	75-82	2-10	89-97	47-49	41-44	79-98	7
8	153-167	83-87	11-16	98-104	50-52	45-47	99-101	8
9	168-180	88-93	17-23	105-112	53-55	48-51	102-107	9
10	181-194	94-99	24-33	113-119	56-59	49-54	108-112	10
11	195-203	100-104	34-39	120-126	60-64	55-58	113-117	11
12	204-221	105-111	40-50	127-136	65-68	59-63	118-126	12
13	222-236	112-121	51-63	137-147	69-79	64-70	127-136	13
14	237-250	122-128	64-72	148-159	80-85	71-77	137-140	14
15	251-267	129-142	73-91	160-179	86-92	78-88	141-161	15
16	268-273	143-164	92-114	180-199	93-103	89-96	162-175	16
17	274-299	165-202	115-161	200-241	104-128	97-105	176-199	17
18	300-306	203-355	162-198	242-356	129-170	106-130	200-314	18
19	307+	356+	199+	357+	171+	131+	315+	19
'N'	284	1147	699	499	217	218	217	'N'
r_{tt}	.98	.93	.93	.95	.89	.89	.91	r_{tt}
C_{90}	2.25	1.19	1.19	1.43	.96	.96	1.05	C_{90}
S.E.M.	6.14	9.32	8.31	10.09	5.70	4.90	7.62	S.E.M.
M.S.D.	12	19	16	20	12	10	15	M.S.D.
MEAN	186.95	99.01	31.33	119.96	61.28	55.03	113.91	MEAN
S.D.	44.32	34.50	31.62	46.33	17.41	14.96	25.34	S.D.

Table 1.9-10 GRADES 9 10

Volume 1. RESPONSE SPEED
Conversion of Raw Scores to Scaled Scores

Scaled Score	ACTIV	PERSIST	AUTOMA-TICITY	AROUSAL NEED	ASSOC INDEX	CODING RATIO	LANG/ABSTRCT	Scaled Score
1	>94	0-8	<(-38)	-0-	0-19	0-9	0-44	1
2	95-110	9-36	(-37)	1-11	20-29	10-24	45-71	2
3	111-129	37-47	(-25)	12-56	30-33	25-27	72-77	3
4	130-143	48-63	(-9)	57-73	34-40	28-30	78-82	4
5	144-158	64-70	(-3)	74-81	41-43	31-37	83-87	5
6	159-163	71-74	(-2)-6	82-88	44-46	38-40	88-91	6
7	164-179	75-82	7-15	89-97	47-49	41-44	79-98	7
8	180-194	83-87	16-22	98-104	50-52	45-47	99-101	8
9	195-208	88-93	23-29	105-112	53-55	48-51	102-107	9
10	209-218	94-99	30-36	113-119	56-59	49-54	108-112	10
11	219-228	100-104	37-44	120-126	60-64	55-58	113-117	11
12	229-240	105-111	45-53	127-136	65-68	59-63	118-126	12
13	241-262	112-121	54-66	137-147	69-79	64-70	127-136	13
14	263-270	122-128	67-75	148-159	80-85	71-77	137-140	14
15	271-288	129-142	76-83	160-179	86-92	78-88	141-161	15
16	289-299	143-164	84-110	180-199	93-103	89-96	162-175	16
17	300-314	165-202	111-142	200-241	104-128	97-105	176-199	17
18	315-319	203-355	143-168	242-356	129-170	106-130	200-314	18
19	320+	356+	169+	357+	171+	131+	315+	19
'N'	284	1147	280	499	217	218	217	'N'
r_{tt}	.96	.93	.95	.95	.89	.89	.91	r_{tt}
C_{90}	1.56	1.19	1.43	1.43	.96	.96	1.05	C_{90}
S.E.M.	6.68	9.32	6.28	10.09	5.70	4.90	7.62	S.E.M.
M.S.D.	14	19	12	20	12	10	15	M.S.D.
MEAN	213.58	99.01	36.21	119.96	61.28	55.03	113.91	MEAN
S.D.	38.96	34.50	27.25	46.33	17.41	14.96	25.34	S.D.

Table 1.11-Adult GRADE 11 - ADULT Volume 1. RESPONSE SPEED
Conversion of Raw Scores to Scaled Scores

Scaled Score	ACTIV	PERSIST	AUTOMA-TICITY	AROUSAL NEED	ASSOC INDEX	CODING RATIO	LANG/ ABSTRCT	Scaled Score
1	>45	0-8	<(-38)	-0-	0-19	0-9	0-44	1
2	46-66	9-36	(-37)	1-11	20-29	10-24	45-71	2
3	67-89	37-47	(-25)	12-56	30-33	25-27	72-77	3
4	90-125	48-63	(-9)	57-73	34-40	28-30	78-82	4
5	126-157	64-70	(-3)	74-81	41-43	31-37	83-87	5
6	158-171	71-74	(-2)-6	82-88	44-46	38-40	88-91	6
7	172-200	75-82	7-15	89-97	47-49	41-44	79-98	7
8	201-215	83-87	16-22	98-104	50-52	45-47	99-101	8
9	216-228	88-93	23-29	105-112	53-55	48-51	102-107	9
10	226-240	94-99	30-36	113-119	56-59	52-54	108-112	10
11	241-258	100-104	37-44	120-126	60-64	55-58	113-117	11
12	259-271	105-111	45-53	127-136	65-68	59-63	118-126	12
13	272-294	112-121	54-66	137-147	69-79	64-70	127-136	13
14	295-308	122-128	67-75	148-159	80-85	71-77	137-140	14
15	309-319	129-142	76-83	160-179	86-92	78-88	141-161	15
16	320-337	143-164	84-110	180-199	93-103	89-96	162-175	16
17	338-353	165-202	111-142	200-241	104-128	97-105	176-199	17
18	354-355	203-355	143-168	242-356	129-170	106-130	200-314	18
19	356+	356+	169+	357+	171+	131+	315+	19
'N'	197	1147	280	499	217	218	217	'N'
r_{tt}	.97	.93	.95	.95	.89	.89	.91	r_{tt}
C_{90}	1.83	1.19	1.43	1.43	.96	.96	1.05	C_{90}
S.E.M.	7.82	9.32	6.28	10.09	5.70	4.90	7.62	S.E.M.
M.S.D.	16	19	12	20	12	10	15	M.S.D.
MEAN	234.96	99.01	36.21	119.96	61.28	55.03	113.91	MEAN
S.D.	50.91	34.50	27.25	46.33	17.41	14.96	25.34	S.D.

Bloomer's Developmental Neuropsychological Assessments (DNA)

Assessing Basic Executive Learning Processes

Volume 1:
Response Speed

Student Response Forms

H

Volume 1 TASK I - LETTER H

N

Volume 1 TASK II - LETTER N

HAT

Volume 1 TASK IV   VARIABLE LETTERS (VARLET)

B	K	D	R	F	I	H	A	I	N	L	F	W	B	K	H	L	A	I	R	K	I	W	N	D	R	K	Z	F	N

A	N	P	I	R	H	Y	K	B	W	X	D	F	F	A	R	E	P	N	Q	W	Z	H	B	Z	R	W	A	M	F

F	H	W	K	Z	I	R	I	H	K	L	R	I	K	I	M	W	K	R	Z	N	L	B	D	K	F	R	I	N	H

I	I	A	L	N	Z	F	T	X	N	B	R	Y	D	R	W	P	H	A	I	F	Z	N	M	V	K	L	R	Z	W

W	T	E	L	X	H	B	K	I	D	R	F	F	P	A	R	E	A	W	Z	N	H	W	B	Z	A	M	R	F	H

Volume 1 TASK V Association Index (ASCINDEX)

1	2	3	4	5	6	7	8	9
F	H	K	R	I	N	B	Z	E

8|3|1|7|9|1|2|8|6|5|4|3|2|6|5|4|7|9|8|6|9|5|7|9|4

1|1|7|5|4|2|3|1|9|4|1|1|3|4|6|3|8|6|4|7|5|2|2|6|3|7

4|2|6|7|3|1|6|5|7|3|9|1|4|2|8|2|5|3|4|7|5|7|6|8|4

2|3|1|7|4|5|3|8|7|4|1|6|4|2|5|8|3|1|7|5|8|1|6|4|7

1|4|2|3|1|1|4|2|5|7|4|6|5|9|2|7|8|9|1|4|8|1|6|2|3|5

Examiner's Work Sheet -Volume 1

Response Speed Variables

CLINICIAN'S WORKSHEET

VARIABLE Learner Name _____ Date _____

Volume 1.   Cognitive Processing Speed

     Measure   Formation   Raw   Total

Scaled

                    Score   Score   Score

1a. ACTIVITY (ACTIVE)
          (LETTER H   ____   ____
     plus LETTERN)   ____   ____   ____

1b. PERSISTENCE (PERSIST)
          ((LETTERN+1)   ____
     divided by (LETTERH+1)*100 ____   ____   ____

1c. AUTOMATICITY (AUTOMAT)
          ((WORDHAT x 3 +1)   ____
     Divided by (LETTERH +1))*100 ____   ____   ____

1d. AROUSAL NEED (AROUSE)
          ((VARLET+1)   ____
     divided by LETTERH+1))*100 ____   ____   ____

CLINICIAN'S WORKSHEET(continued)

Measure	Formation	Raw Score	Total Score	Scaled Score

1e. PAIRED-ASSOCIATION INDEX (PAINDX)

$((ASCINDEX+1)$ ____

divided by $LETTERH+1))*100$ ____ ____   ____

1f. CODING RATIO (CODERATO)

$(WISC-III CODING+1)$ ____

divided by $LETTERH+1))*100$ ____ ____   ____

1g. LANGUAGE/ABSTRACT PROCESSING (LANG/ABS)

$((ASOCINDEX+1)$ ____

Divided by WISC CODING$+1))*100$____ ____   ____

www.ingramcontent.com/pod-product-compliance
Lightning Source LLC
Chambersburg PA
CBHW070251290326
41930CB00041B/2453